THE BEST OF

SURVIVORS FROM SOUTH POLE BUS FOUND

SPHERE BOOKS LIMITED

A SPHERE BOOK

First published in Great Britain 1989 by
Sphere Books Ltd

Copyright © Sunday Sport 1989

ISBN 0 7474 0561 1

Reproduced, printed and bound in Great Britain
by Hazell, Watson & Viney, Aylesbury, Bucks.

Sphere Books Ltd
A Division of
Macdonald & Co (Publishers) Ltd
27 Wrights Lane, London W8 5TZ
A member of Maxwell Pergamon Publishing Corporation plc

HOW TO TELL IF YOUR MUM-IN-LAW IS AN ALIEN

Intergalactic exclusive

SPECIAL INVESTIGATION By SIMON FINLAY

NEXT time your misery-guts mother-in-law bends your ear . . . just take a look at HERS.

For those jug-lugs which can pick up a juicy titbit of gossip from 200 paces could prove she's an ALIEN!

Even fellas with girlfriends who have small but perfectly-formed boobs, like gorgeous Gaynor Goodman (left), had better watch out — because they TOO could be human ETs.

But don't despair — a top boffin has revealed an easy guide to spotting aliens in the street, which our leggy lovely couldn't wait to illustrate.

"It's quite simple to identify aliens when you know the features to look for," said UFO expert Henri Noblet.

His tell-tale inter-galactic signs include:

● Large green or hazel eyes set far apart
● Long, slender hands and fingers
● Small feet and long toes
● Firm, muscular thighs

Henri's views for spotting closet aliens have been taken seriously by the world's elite UFOlogists . . . who say loads of Brits could have inter-planetary blood.

"A definite sudden change did take place on this planet 8,000 years ago and natural selection and evolution is too slow to have caused it," said German archaeologist Dr Richard Graf.

"It is likely it came about by the introduction of superior characteristics from extra-terrestrial genes."

Rex Dutta, director of Britain's leading UFO magazine, Viewpoint Aquarius, agrees with Noblet.

Recognition

"Our planet has always been mixing with other life forms. Just because we haven't been to distant planets it doesn't mean we haven't been visited," he said.

Rex also claimed alien descendants have telepathic powers and are singled out by visiting extra-terrestrials who recognise their own kin.

"They are likely to hold positions of power or work in caring professions."

■A FOOT-FETISH fiend was put behind bars after sucking the toes of unsuspecting women.

The loony pounced on 30 women in banks and supermarkets and asked them if he could touch their feet.

One California girl cop said: "I never wear open-toed shoes in supermarkets anymore."

STINKING SOCK CHOKES SOCCER FAN

Attack of the killer clobber

ASTONISHED soccer fan Alec Cruickshank didn't believe the old wives tale about cheesey socks walking by themselves... until one tried to **STRANGLE** him.

For when one of Alec's socks caught sight of the laundry basket it almost killed him in a frenzied attempt to escape a dip in soapy water.

The ordeal began when slap-happy Alec put smelly knee-length socks — which hadn't been washed for SIX weeks — in for a soak.

But when the West Ham fan turned his back, the festering footwear sprang to life and:

- **FORCED** the lid off the laundry basket.
- **SOARED** through the air.
- **WRAPPED** itself around Alec's neck and tried to strangle him.

"At first I didn't realise what was happening. I hadn't been up very long," said 17-year-old Alec.

"I thought I'd disturbed a burglar until I saw myself in the mirror. It was like something

SHOCK ... Alec

out of a horror film. The sock was trying to STRANGLE me," he said.

Alien rain hits Earth

SNOW joke! Scientists believe that giant snowballs may be bombarding the Earth — from SPACE.

The massive chunks made of ice and dust are thought to be fragments of comets.

Each year an estimated ten MILLION rain down on the Earth's atmosphere.

Oceans

And the water from them could have produced all the oceans on the planet.

An expert said: "It's a nice theory. This could be one of the major discoveries of the decade.

"We have to hope it doesn't go on, though, or we'll all be flooded out."

D.I.Y. HUBBY STUFFS WIFE DOWN PLUGHOLE

By RAY LEVINE

BLOODTHIRSTY killer Thomas Fisher settled a lovers' tiff with his pretty wife Babs by flushing her down the PLUGHOLE!

Bloodbath as monster goes round the U-bend

DIRTY TRICK!

DANCER Mavisa Lonez, of Chile, was charged with indecency during her act, so she performed it in court to applause from the jury . . . which found her guilty.

KILLER SPIRIT MEETS MATCH

FORMER US Air Force servicemen meet tomorrow at an abandoned air base in Kent to exorcise the ghost of a GI haunting the sergeants' mess.

They hope to expel the spirit of Napoleon Green from Marston Airfield where he committed suicided after slaughtering three and wounding seven comrades.

TOT LIVES 4 YEARS ON SINGLE BAKED BEAN

AMAZING tot Kimberley Daggit has survived four years on a SINGLE BAKED BEAN.

The fragile toddler broke her bizarre fast just ONCE for the cold morsel — and took half an hour to eat it.

Now Kimberley's worried mum Janice believes she may have reared the world's first anorexic baby.

"I just can't understand it, but whatever I give Kimberley she pushes away in horror," said Janice, 33.

"It was a miracle when we got that single bean down her.

"The worst thing is I can see she's hungry. Her eyes are crying our for food but something inside her says NO.

"It's just like the slimming disease anorexia nervosa."

Baffled docs can't work out why the fragile four-year-old loves watching other people eat but won't touch a scrap herself.

Physically she's perfect — and although she's half the size she should be, Kimberley's full of life.

Strangely, she adores seeing her mum scoff a cream cake and wanders around the house with a packet of crisps which she doles out to her brothers and sisters.

Kimberley even watches her mum cooking and licks her lips when dinner's on the boil.

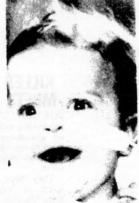

FAST . . . Kimberley

"Nevertheless she gets in a right state if I put something solid in front of her," said ex-teacher Janice.

"She almost has a fit and won't even open her mouth. I know deep down she's dying for food, she's starving but there's some sort of block in her mind."

According to Dr Peter Milla, a stomach specialist at London's Great Ormond Street Children's Hospital, the medical world is stumped by the strange fast.

Actress fights off alien sex spy

OSCAR-WINNING actress Sandy Dennis last night told how she was spied in the nude . . . by a peeping-tom ALIEN!

For when the star peeled off her clothes she didn't realise she was giving an impromptu strip show for sex-starved spacemen.

"I was undressing one night and looking out of my window I could see lots of tiny green lights moving about between the trees," said Sandy, star of The Fox and Who's Afraid Of Virginia Woolf?

Pervies

When the astonished 51-year-old actress dashed to investigate she found the interplanetary pervies had scarpered back to their spacecraft.

The warped space travellers then used an invisible beam to try to such her into the ship.

Sandy recalled: "I really had to fight to **free** my will."

WORLD'S LAZIEST SLOB LIES IN BED FOR 56 YEARS

EASY-GOING John Richards last night claimed the title SUPER SLOB . . . after staying in bed for an incredible 56 YEARS!

Bone idle John, who never did a day's work in his life, turned in for a kip in 1932 and hasn't bothered to get up since.

The champion skiver was just 16 when he announced to his stunned family: "I'm going upstairs — I may be some time."

Now aged 72, John has SNORED through ten governments; KIPPED while men landed on the moon and DOZED through a world war.

So fur, so good

A SHOCKED motorist found the purr under the bonnet was not coming from the engine .

The moggy jumped out unharmed when the driver stopped at a County Durham garage after a 100-mile journey from Scotland.

GIANT SPROUT FROM OUTER SPACE ATE MY PAL

A GIANT green sprout from Venus turned killer when it beamed down on to milkman Dave Smith's garden.

For the violent vegetable from outer space caused chaos in the cabbage patch where Dave was busy weeding.

In an extra-terrestrial orgy of destruction the sinister sprout GOBBLED its way through a row of runner-beans, TRAMPLED all over his prize tomatoes, SQUASHED his strawberry plants flat and MARCHED all over his prize marrows.

Then the football-sized space fiend launched a horrifying attack on Dave's best mate, Steve Jones.

"I was terrified out of my mind," admitted Dave as he recovered from his ordeal at home in Wiggington, Tamworth, Staffs.

The pals had just moved into their new house, and Dave was clearing a wild, overgrown area at the bottom of the garden.

Humming

"I heard a rustling in the undergrowth and when I turned around there was this giant sprout jumping up and down like a space-hopper," said Dave, 28.

TERRIFIED . . . Dave

UFO bun stole my knickers

SWEET-TOOTHED cake shop worker Fatma Mahaat nearly died of fright when an alien meringue zoomed up her pinny.

For the cream cake Fatma dropped on the floor by mistake was no sweet treat — but a UFO battleship that invaded her knickers.

The cunningly disguised inter-galactic visitor had been laying low in a cake tray say experts.

"When I dropped it. it sort of whirred to life," said Fatma, 21, of Bitlis, Turkey.

"Then it lifted itself above the floor and went for me.

"The next thing I knew, the meringue was whooshing under my pinny. It came out with my undies draped over its shell and flew out the door!"

Local alien expert, Yilmaz Salih, said "We are getting more and more reports of UFO's taking on the form of common food items for safety.

"It is possible they are alien battlecruisers."

SURVIVORS FROM SOUTH POLE BUS FOUND

Green alien driver got lost in London

SURVIVORS from the London double-decker bus found in the frozen South Pole told last night of their nightmare journey to the Antarctic.

We've been SNOWED under with letters giving CHILLING accounts of the drama — which prove an ALIEN drove the ill-fated Number 109 to the ice-cap in 1961.

"I was on that bus and I remember clearly how they changed the crew. A little green man got on and we went on a sort of helter-skelter journey to the South Pole," revealed Stan Williams, 53.

Sunday Sport last week told the world how the bus pulled out of Croydon Bus Garage in Surrey 28 years ago . . . only to be found buried up to its front-axle in a glacier.

But airport worker Stan thanked his favourite Sunday paper for SAVING his marriage.

"I went missing for two days and my wife Sheila didn't believe my story until she saw the piece in Sunday Sport," he said from his home in Horley, Surrey.

"She thought I'd been out drinking with my mates or had another woman on the go."

The doting husband told how he boarded the 109 in Streatham on his way to work in Central London.

"This little green chap

TIME WARP . . . Sid

LEAK . . . for Hugh

PASSENGER...Stan

FREEZE FRAME . our exclusive picture of the 109 which ended up at the South Pole after being hijacked by an alien

By SIMON FINLAY

called Oates announced he was driving the bus and asked me for the fare," Stan remembered.

"I was a little frightened because he was ugly with a pointed nose and peculiar ears, but I still refused to pay.

"I don't remember much of the South Pole except seeing lots of ice.

"The next thing I remember was finding myself in Brixton High Street covered in ice."

Barman Joe Pearson is CONVINCED his missing granny was on the 109.

"She had her will in her handbag and we reckon she was worth at least £50 million — so obviously we are very concerned," said Joe, 52.

"Now we fear she might have turned into a penguin because she went to London Zoo every Sunday to feed them sardines."

Salesman

Mature student John La Trobe revealed how he caught the double-decker.

"In 1961, I was a poor muesli salesman trying to sell my wares in London. The whole journey is a complete blank, but I do remember the penguins," said John.

Star wars as US aces fight aliens

U.S. fighter pilots have been flying on suicide missions to destroy invading alien warships, a secret White House dossier has revealed.

According to informed Pentagon sources, the airmen have been chasing fleets of flying saucers – under orders from the CIA.

None of the pilots or craft has ever returned after the Star Wars battles.

Barry Greenwood, boss of the Citizens Against UFO Secrecy movement, said last night: "If pilots are disappearing under such circumstances we want to know about it. There must not be a cover up."

3 INCH DOG ATE MY MISSUS

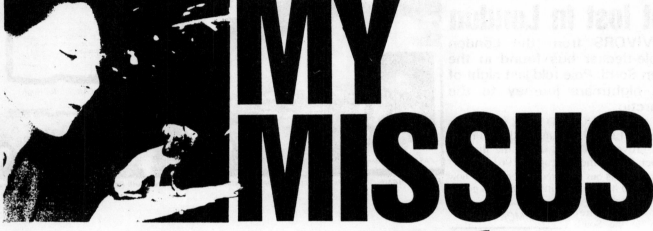

● JAWS ... tiny Tinkerbell did more than just bite the hand that fed her — she ate owner Theresa's arm and body

By JACK CANT following up a lead in Tokyo

ANIMAL-LOVER Theresa Wolem thought she had the perfect pet in the world's smallest dog ... until it ATE her.

Boffins have vowed to destroy the new breed of Frankenstein pooches after inventing three-inch dogs that turn into KILLERS.

Tragic Theresa's heart-break hubby told last night how he came home to find their pint-sized pet, Tinkerbell, GUZZLING his missus.

"There wasn't much left by then — just her ring finger, and that was bigger than the dog," wept distraught Marty Wolem.

The family had only just bought the space-age mutt the week before from Japan's top secret Kobayaschi Canine Research Centre.

"I fell to the floor and pulled at the finger with blood spurting over my hand. But Tinkerbell's jaws were locked hard," cried Marty.

"It chewed through that finger in a frenzy like a piranha fish until I had to drop it for fear of losing MY hand."

Scientists fear Tinkerbell — the first of a type of Tinka dog — went for

28-year-old Theresa's throat after suddenly turning savage.

"Theresa loved that dog and cradled it to her bosom like a baby. But I was always wary of its amazingly loud growl," remembered Marty, 39.

It took scientists in Tokyo FIVE years to develop a litter of dogs like six-ounce Tinkerbell, a genetic freak cross-bred to behave like a guard dog and fit in a matchbox.

Crossbred

"The Tinka was crossbred from dachshund and dobermans. It's as vicious as any attack-dog and tiny as a mouse," explained genetic vet Dr Katsumi Taguchi in Tokyo.

"Japan is very overcrowded with houses too small for normal-sized guard dogs, so we intented a compact animal.

"Like all things in Japan, it is as big, bad and vicious as any Western alternative, but fits in the pockets.

"Unfortunately, Tinkerbell

HUBBY TURNS WIFE INTO EGYPTIAN MUMMY

MUMMY'S BOY... Alf wants life after death, and (inset) his pyramid

By RAY LEVINE

KING Tut nut Alf Greco told last night of his bizarre bid to bring his family back to life by turning them into Egyptian MUMMIES.

The loopy librarian, wife Janet and son Jeremy will all be PICKLED — and banged up in special bronze cases when they die.

And in a walking mummy horror, they're hoping they will come back from the dead once boffins find a way a CLONE human beings.

"If scientists are right, they will be able to bring us back to life after we die," exclaimed 15-year-old son Jeremy.

"Experts say in 50 years they'll be able to clone people from the blood's DNA cells, which are perfectly preserved during mummification."

During the macabre £7,700 treatment, Janet will have her innards pulled out and pickled in preserving jars... while the rest of her body stews in a tank of embalming fluid.

After three weeks her vital organs will be replaced before she is wrapped in a modern-day plastic bandage and shut away in a bronze mummy case.

"It's all deadly serious. Anyone who took the time to think about it would be mummified too," said Alf.

"Apart from the exciting possibility of being re-born, does the thought of being incinerated or eaten by maggots when you die appeal to you?" he demanded.

The barmy bookworm is just one of a hundred people who have signed a contract with crazy embalmer Corky Raa to have the King Tut treatment when they die.

The 44-year-old madcap mortician, from Salt Lake City, Utah, is the boss of the Summon Society — who hold the world's only patent for mummification.

Alf has already shelled out a staggering £40,000 to Corky, who mummified the family's pet dog and entombed it in a PYRAMID.

And the treaky 40-year-old father's family are firmly behind his bizarre burial plan.

● MUMMY MAN Corky Raa started working like an ancient Egyptian 14 years ago.

A hundred people have already coughed up £7,700 for him to preserve their bodies in the style of the Pharaohs.

I HAD 40 MEN IN A NIGHT

Gloria claims she played the hornpipe with an entire ship's crew

GOOD-TIME GIRL Gloria Lovatt yesterday revealed how her ship really did come in ... when she bonked an entire 40-man crew in one night.

The saucy sailors were QUEUEING UP to take their turn with the Liverpool lovely after word of her sex-ploits got round town.

And last night Gloria confessed: "They all had me in just under four hours.

"The whole ship's company wanted me. At first I thought I would never manage them all — but I did.

"It was the best night I ever had because they were great lovers. I satisfied them all and told them they could look me up when they hit town again."

Green-fingered aliens shocker

SHOCKED gran Jean Coolsting told last night how green-fingered aliens beamed down to work on her garden.

Jean, 62, says a blazing UFO hovered outside her bedroom windows and sprayed intergalactic fertiliser over her flowers and trimmed her favourite dahlias.

"I got up in the morning and there was a strange, mist like liquid all over the lawn and bushes," said the hospital worker from Camberley, Surrey.

"As for as I know, it was a deposit from the spaceship and, believe it or not, this has happened before.

"Our family must attract them . . . we've had 20 UFO sightings between us.

"On the visit in question they had a strange effect on the greenery. It helped the flowers grow."

Remembrance Day shocker

HITLER FOUND ALIVE

REBORN ... Hitler scourge of Germany

By SIMON FINLAY

NAZI butcher Adolf Hitler is ALIVE and back in Germany, we can reveal this Remembrance Day morning.

Almost half a century since the end of the war, the Beast of Berlin has been reincarnated in the body of German housepainter Robert Schneller.

Britain's war heroes — today honouring their dead comrades at the Cenotaph — will weep after seeing our pictures of the reborn Führer.

Since he was a boy, Schneller, now 52, increasingly talked, walked, thought and looked like the Führer, until now he accepts his awful fate.

"I can't resist him. I am possessed by Hitler's spirit. I have become Hitler," wept Schneller at his home in the Feurbach suburb of Stuttgart.

"The most evil and hated man in the history of the world has been reborn in me. Please, God, help me!"

Nasty Nazi reincarnated as painter

EXCLUSIVE

Dr. WHO'S DALEK WAS MY RED HOT LOVER

'Sex with him's a pleasure'

DALEK . . . lover for Irena.

By SIMON FINLAY

HORNY housewife Irena Weeks revealed last night she's been sharing her bed with a DALEK for 12 years!

Speaking for the first time about her bizarre marriage to the 5ft-high metal monster with a deadly antenna, Irena said her hubby is the spitting image of Dr Who's evil TV foe.

"I have been living with a Dalek for years. He's been very good to me," said Irena.

As the BBC drama celebrates 25 years on TV, Irena admitted she's still very much in love with her husband, who never stops chanting: "EXTERMINATE, EXTERMINATE!!"

And she confessed the metal meanie rolls around the bedroom waiting to give her Dalek-style sex thrills.

"He's not at all sinister. Sex with him is very physical — but it's also very pleasurable," revealed Irena.

And the 34-year-old former artist is kept satisfied by him on a ration of TWO Dalek bonks a week.

"He is kept so busy with his missions, but it is enough for me".

But stunned Dr Who Appreciation Society expert Andrew Beech said: "It's most strange. I have never heard of this type of thing before."

Ever since she fell in love with her dirty Dalek in 1976, Irena claims that she has never been attracted to human hunks.

The Dalek even got her PREGNANT but dissolved the foetus after three weeks. "He injected a serum into my arm near the elbow, but then he inserted another one a few days later to end my pregnancy."

But Irena confessed that sex with her hubby leaves her hungry. "I feel fine afterwards but a little peckish. Not hungry for more — just for food!"

Watching

Irena, who used to be married to a naval officer and lives in Barrington, Rhode Island, USA, claims her husband magically appeared in her home one day, saying that he had been "watching" her for years.

"He said that I was worthy to be his bride and, of course, I accepted," said Irena.

Irena admitted that her "man" is on a mission to EXTERMINATE evil from the universe.

She said the rolling robot is really a "witty and charming" alien — unlike the devious Daleks in the BBC blockbuster.

"He trusts me and I will always stay with him. He is my guardian and my friend."

Kickabout ball was a UFO

A FOOTBALL-shaped UFO from Venus has put soccer mad builder Jim Wilson in an astronomical spin.

For burly JCB driver Jim almost started a kick around with ET when the glowing intergalactic off-side bounced down his road.

"It was the oddest thing I've ever seen and I must admit it was certainly frightening at first," said Jim, 40.

Now the sighting has kicked off amazing speculation that the extra-terrestrial visitor could be from Venus!

"It was about a foot wide and was shaped like a football," said Mike Hanson, Director of International Research for the Yorkshire UFO Society, after investigating Jim's sighting.

"It came from the Northern sky — the planet Venus is just slightly to the West of that part of space," he said.

By GARY THOMPSON

Father-of-two Jim was scraping ice from the windscreen of his car at his home in Rotherham, Yorkshire, when he saw the spaceball.

Sparks

He watched goggle eyed as it bounced down the street spewing out sparks before DISAPPEARING into thin air.

Defence chiefs have now launched a probe into the sighting. And a spokesman at RAF Finningly near Doncaster described the alien ball as "puzzling" and said a report would be drawn up.

MY ALSATIAN IS A LAGER LOUT

Pilot was grabbed by aliens

A YOUNG pilot, who vanished in mid-air being chased by a cigar-shaped object, was seized by ALIENS, experts revealed last night.

Their sensational findings show that 20-year-old Frederick Valentich was abducted on a flight from Melbourne to a nearby island.

Now 11 years later NASA physicist and author Richard Haines says he has proof that aliens were responsible.

The experts heard a recording of Valentich's chilling last message to Air Traffic Control.

"It is a long shape with a green light. And it is metallic-like, all shiny," he said.

In his book The Melbourne Episode — Case Study of a Missing Pilot, Haines says the pilot started panicking and shouted: "That strange aircraft is hovering over me again."

GET THEM IN... half-cut Holly

HALF-CUT hound Holly was in the doghouse last night... for being a LAGER LOUT!

The boozy bitch's fed-up owner, Colin Bramble, is going bonkers over his dog's drinking.

Alcoholic Ale-sation Holly guzzles gallons of brain-warping beer and turns into a rowdy raver.

The legless two-and-a-half year old poochy regularly: PINCHES Colin's pints, SPITS all over the floor, STAGGERS about crashing into tables, and NURSES a stinking HANGOVER after her ale-swilling sessions.

"She sticks her tongue in my pint and nicks the beer," said Colin.

"Then she slobbers all over the place like a drunken lager lout."

The tanked-up German Shepherd is so hooked on booze that she refuses to go WALKIES without loads of DRINKIES!

Problem

Every time Colin, 44, takes Holly out for a pee, she drags him down to their local for the hair of the dog.

"I take her down to the

By BRANDON MALINSKY

woods and she pulls me along to the pub. I can't stop her," said Colin.

"When we get there, she makes it known that she wants a drink — and then she dives into my pint."

The mad mutt's drink problem got so bad that Colin feared she'd snuff it with a lousy liver.

"She'd down about three pints a night and start WOBBLING about in a bad way," he said.

"Then she'd go and lie down afterwards. And she always wakes up with a headache.

"I made her ease up on her drinking because I thought she was going to get liver disease. Now she can take her drink much better."

Holly first had a tipple when Colin, from Cosham, near Portsmouth, ran a pub.

"She would empty the drip trays at the end of the night, even if there was a good few pints in them," said Colin, a father of two.

Partners

These days, the unlikely drinking partners regularly share a few pints at their favourite boozer, The Portsbridge, in Cosham.

"She loves her beer and if I let her, she would drink until she collapsed," said Colin.

But he warned that Holly would not be so JOLLY if a burglar had the FOLLY to go after Colin's LOLLY.

"She's a great guard dog and anybody would be stupid to try and break in when Holly's behind the door," he said.

CASE CLOTHED

POLICE who swooped on a beach in Redwood City, California, failed to catch any nudists who were illegally frolicking there — but they did arrest 33 Peeping Toms.

ASH CASH

A Philadelphia woman who banned her husband from smoking cigars at home has been left £1 million in his will — on condition she smokes six cheroots a day.

IT'S YOUR PIG OR ME

FARMER'S wife Nola Schey has caused a right stink — by sharing a bed with her hubby Don and a 70-stone porker called Spot.

For the mixed-up missus has fallen for a brown and white bachelor — and he's a real PIG!

Even when her fed-up husband stormed: "It's the hog or me!" Nola insisted on keeping BOTH.

And yesterday, when she spoke for the first time of their incredible pig-in-the-middle marriage, she admitted: "I wouldn't like Don to hear it, but Spot would have made a better husband. It nearly broke us up but now I'm happy to say I've got them both."

When it's time for sex, the pot-bellied porker makes his excuses and LEAVES. But, just like a hunpecked hubby, Spot enjoys:

OINK! Tea on the table at six — usually meat and two veg followed by ice cream;

SNORT! His own space on the sofa — where he watches his favourite TV show Hill Street Blues with Nola;

GRUNT! Getting his back scrubbed in the farming family's giant bath.

"At first I was really jealous that my wife wanted to move the pig into our bed," blushed Don, 40.

"I tried to kick him out into the pen in the yard but he just kept coming back.

"I even decorated another bedroom for Spot to sleep in but if he's left on his own he just gets lonely and waddles down to us in the middle of the night.

"At first we'd try to get him back to his own bed because there was no space for us but we gave up. If he doesn't want to budge he won't and that's all there is to it."

In an incredible about-turn, Don decided: "If you can't beat 'em, join em!"

And now he confesses he learned his lesson when his pretty brunette wife said she would rather have the hog.

"I've been a bit of a swine myself," said Don, "so I've decided that from now on Spot can hog the duvet as much as he likes.

"We're like one big happy family. I've even got accustomed to having Spot sleep between us and I can't imagine it without him.

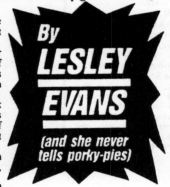

By LESLEY EVANS
(and she never tells porky-pies)

"We recommend a hog to anyone for a sleeping partner — Nola and I find him really affectionate, warm and cuddly.

"In fact I know she'd rather have him than me because I snore louder."

Playing in the tub

Curvy Nola, 37, reckons pigs can be much better hubbles than your average fella.

She even shares the bath tub with the pet porker.

"I love playing around in the tub with Spot. I always give him a rub down after me. He has more baths than my husband," said Nola.

"At least he doesn't leave his smelly socks around," she said.

Snap!

FOUR seamen appeared before a Buenos Aires court after fighting over the same woman. Each carried an autographed photo of her.

When the magistrate saw the picture he burst into tears and rushed out. It was his wife.

PIG

AMAZINGLY, pigs are the only mammals, apart from humans, which get voluntarily drunk. They are known to get tipsy gorging rotting, fermenting windfalls in apple-orchards.

SPOT

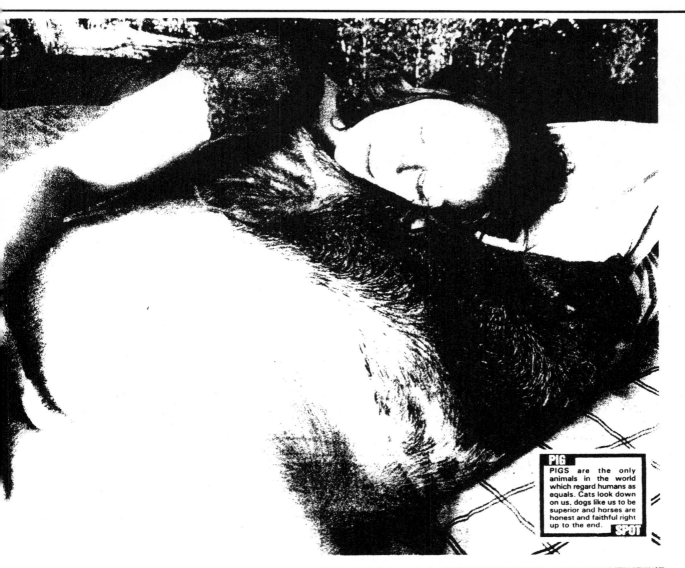

Charles tells of lav love

PRINCE Charles revealed last night why he spends so much time at Sandringham ...it's got the best BOGS!

For the loo–loving Royal practises for when he takes the THRONE by sitting on the posh estate's LAVVIE.

"Apart from anything else, it's got the best bathrooms in the business," he told sexy Selina Scott in an interview on American television.

Palace insiders say Charles – who also told Selina he knows what he's talking about when he expresses an opinion – has always prided himself on the state of the Royal KAZI.

"He believes toilets are an important part of what helps make Britain GREAT," said our source.

LOO–NY... Charlie

TIGHT SQUEEZE... Spot, Nola and Don get some shut-eye

GUN-TOTING GRANDAD DOES BUNK ON BIKE

World's oldest bandit

GERIATRIC bank-robber Jack Kelm was behind bars last night . . . after trying to escape cops on his PUSHBIKE!

The gun-toting grandad — the world's oldest practising villain at 82 — was nabbed wearing a stocking over his head as he frantically pedalled down a high street.

And now former neighbourhood nice guy Jack — whose tangle with the law has stunned fellow old codgers — is prime suspect in another TEN robbery cases.

By MARTIN TURNER

"So far as our records go, he's probably the oldest bandit about," said amazed cop Richard Schussler.

"They can't come much older, can they."

OAP Jack, who told cops he turned to crime because he couldn't afford to live on his measly pension, used his rusty old pushbike as a getaway vehicle because he hasn't got a motor.

But the frail old duffer didn't have enough pedal power as he made off with swag from a bank in Colorado — and was captured by an eye witness who chased after him ON FOOT.

Now Kelm, who kept a string of previous convictions secret from pals — is being held

VILLAIN . . . on a pension

in custody in Denver, Colorado, awaiting trial.

FBI men say they've uncovered Jack's dark past — and revealed he's already served prison sentences for other robberies.

"The man wore two faces," revealed agent Schussler.

"One, as the humanitarian who'd got out of his way to help people in the town of Greeley, where he lived, and another when he wanted to rob a bank."

Friends say they had no idea pensioner Jack led a secret life as an arch-villain.

"We cannot believe old Jack would do such a thing. He was the most wonderful person in our town," said mother-of-two Michele Terriere.

"He would buy food and presents for the local children,

tended the gardens of the elderly and even walked the sick to hospital.

"If he ever had any cash to spare, he'd buy bread to feed the ducks in the park. That's the generous sort of man he was."

And churchworker Joanee Truitt added: "I'm staggered. He did odd jobs in the church

and there wasn't a person who did not like him."

But cops are adamant they've got their man.

"Kelm may be an old guy but he's also a criminal," said Sgt Tom McLellan of Fort Collins nick.

"During the various robberies Kelm has pointed a weapon at lots of people, many of them women, and they were terrified."

He carried out his first robbery in Illinois in 1921 and committed more in Colorado and Florida.

The old lag kept the long arm of the law busy in the succeeding years by escaping from prisons in various states including fleeing from a chain gang in 1936.

Angry alien kicked habit

A GRUMPY alien who quit smoking for his New Year's resolution has gone on a tobacco shop rampage. The reformed smoker beamed himself down to Earth, determined to exact revenge on the planet that invented smoking.

- KA-POW! He smashed fag cartons to pieces;
- ZAP! He blasted pipes out of pensioners' mouths;
- ZONK! His laser-beam eyes turned tobacco fields to smouldering stubble.

"It was horrific. The alien was a miserable-looking monster with a rasping smoker's cough," said eye-witness Calo Bugliso in Charleston, West Virginia, USA.

"He zapped through the tobacco fields growling that he'd kicked the habit for the New Year.

"And he said that if it hadn't been for Sir Walter Raleigh discovering the stuff on Earth in the first place, he would never have started."

Police refused to confirm reports of large-scale alien lout damage in the tobacco state, but anti-smoking group ASH said they were delighted at the news.

PACKET . . . of trouble

VAMPIRES ATTACK MAN WATCHING HORROR MOVIE

A BANKER is suing a crazed gang of 20 VAMPIRES who stormed into his flat and bit him while he was watching a TV Dracula movie.

Conrad Herman claims the gnashing ghouls sank their fangs into him 26 times before he leapt through a first floor window to escape and broke three ribs.

He was bitten 26 times before leaping out of window

Legal papers filed before a court in his home town Liege, Belgium, request unspecified damages to compensate 48-year-old Conrad for his "mental and physical trauma".

"A lot of people think my lawsuit is one big joke. But I'm

By BILL CORKE

deadly serious," said the batty banker.

"Those maniacs kicked down the door of my apartment and tried to eat me alive in my own living room while I was watching television.

Killed

"They were biting me with their fangs, and clawing me like a bunch of wild animals.

"I really thought they were going to kill me — and they would have done if I hadn't got away. It's a miracle I'm still here to talk about it."

Conrad told police he wounded — or possibly killed — three of the vampires with a metal poker, although no bodies have been recovered.

Amazingly, detectives believe Conrad's story because the walls of his flat were splattered with blood

GOOD TASTE

A FRENCH delicatessen took out a newspaper advert congratulating a burglar on his taste after he stole only the best food from the shop in a smash and grab raid.

when they arrived to investigate.

"We've had dealings with these vampires before," police lieutenant Hugo Zeegers admitted.

"If Mr Herman did wound or kill any of them, I'm sure this gang would have taken the bodies with them.

"They're a close-knit bunch and we want to question them about dozens of similar attacks in this region.

"We know their names, but so far we've been unable to track them down."

In an unusual legal move, Conrad's lawyer is to ask a judge to hear the case in the absence of the vampire gang.

Vicious

"I want a ruling on this case as soon as possible," said lawyer Jane Moureau.

"It's vital the jurors see Mr Herman's bite marks and bandages so they'll know just how vicious these monsters really are.

Conrad added: "It's the most horrific thing that's ever happened to me.

"It's certainly something I could never have made up in my wildest dreams — and it's certainly something I will never forget.

Dog gone it... he's pickled

YOUNG Jeremy Greco plays with his pet Dobermann Butch every day... even though the dog's been DEAD for a year.

For mum Janet turned the family pet into a mummified mutt after he died of old age last winter.

And when school finishes, Jeremy catches a bus to Corky Raa's pyramid in Salt Lake City, Utah, to play imaginary games with the pampered pooch.

"Mom saw how upset I was when Butch died and she thought it would be nice to have him mummified," said Jeremy.

BUTCH... pickled

CHUCK'S AWAY!

A PLANE in Dallas, Texas, flew by itself for two hours after its pilot, 27-year-old Chuck Selley was catapulted out while making a bumpy landing.

STAR BRAS

THE wackiest museum in the world has opened in Hollywood . . . dedicated to bras from the stars and featuring exhibits from big-busted Madonna and Phyllis Diller.

VIRGIN MARY BUILT OUR SHED

DIY miracle shocker

Holding hands

LOVESICK jailbird Mitch King couldn't bear to be parted from his wife — so he stuck himself to her with superglue!

Handcuffed to a warder, they were whisked off to hospital in Auckland, New Zealand for a vigorous 90-minute scrubbing session to separate them.

A GOB-SMACKED farmer's wife watched in amazement as the VIRGIN MARY came down from Heaven . . . to mend her hubby's SHED.

For, when softly-spoken Despina Pavlou's family decided to convert a tin shack on their small sheep farm into a homemade church, they witnessed a D.I.Y. miracle.

As a brow-beaten chippie ran into problems with his plywood, the Madonna lent a helping hand by BANGING in nails and fitting a wooden panel to the wall.

And while stunned clergymen were racking their brains last night, Despina's son Paul told of how his mum is now in DAILY contact with the Virgin Mary.

"The carpenter was having some problems trying to fit some plywood to the wall," revealed Paul, 29.

"He couldn't get the nails in and was having difficulty cutting it to size — then the Holy Mother helped him.

"He turned away and suddenly the work was done. My mum thought it was AMUSING because the Holy Mother did it with such ease."

Ticking off from Jesus!

DEVOUT Christian Paul Pavlou claims to have met Jesus on his dad's sheep farm. Christ has visited at least TEN times, he says.

"He appeared two-and-a-half years after Despina first saw the Holy Mother," revealed Paul.

Amazingly, Christ visited 53-year-old Despina to give her a TICKING-OFF for asking the Virgin Mary too many questions.

He said: "My mother will tell you what she needs to tell you" claimed Paul. "He also appeared and said 'I am the light' three times. The whole time, light was shining from him like nothing I have ever seen."

Paul says Jesus Mary BOTH appeared before his family when construction on their church first began.

2-HEADED SANTA EATS HIS REINDEER

EXCLUSIVE TO SLEIGH THE REST

By *CHRISTINE RODERICK*

SANTA CLAUS was last night exposed as a two-headed MONSTER after gobbling up Rudolph the Red-nosed Reindeer in a food frenzy.

Our exclusive pictures show Santa minutes after he scoffed Rudolph whole ... then washed him down with a pint.

The shock revelation that Santa is a mutant GLUTTON will leave millions of children in tears this Christmas Eve.

"It's terrible. The kids will be crying into their cornflakes," said top kiddies' TV presenter Philip Schofield.

"I always thought Rudolph was indestructable. His death will ruin every kid's Christmas in Britain."

But Philip could not rule out the possibility that Santa was born with TWO heads.

"Every Christmas I sit up for hours waiting for Santa to come," admitted the heart-throb Going Live host.

"But I'm always asleep by the time he arrives. You never know, the REAL Santa may very well have two heads.

BOIL IN A BAG GIRL LIVES IN FRIDGE

ANOTHER RED HOT EXCLUSIVE

HOT TOT ... Frances and her special suit

NASA scientists devise cool outfit for tragic Frances

FIERY schoolgirl Frances Ott has been branded the world's first boil-in-the-bag youngster because of the bizarre plastic suit she wears to prevent overheating.

A rare medical condition means she just can't control her body heat, and when temperatures outside soar, little Frances has STEAM coming out of her ears.

The human radiator, who blows the tops off thermometers, could never play in the sun like other kiddies — until now.

For top space scientists have designed an incredible portable fridge she can strap to her back to cool her down.

The wacky outfit works like a giant ice pack and needs topping up every two hours . . . otherwise seven-year-old Frances would literally boil in the bag.

"We have to be careful that the suit is recharged or it would backfire and the plastic lining would cause her to overheat instead of cooling her down," explained mum Nancy.

Frail Frances, who stunned medics by sending mercury in thermometers shooting over the 105F mark, is the first ever gas-cooled child.

Her amazing NASA-designed vest and helmet pump freon gas around her small frame and stop her from burning up.

Loo on view

A LOO from the former home of Sir Harry Secombe is set to become a permanent exhibit in a museum.

The potty plan was launched by local councillor, Glyn Sparkes, when he heard the two-tone buff and white loo had been removed during renovations from Sir Harry's old house in Swansea.

Now the city's Industrial and Maritime Museum will show off Sir Harry's former family seat.

LOVESICK GARDENER MARRIES LETTUCE

GARDENER Steve Mahon became so proud of his prize lettuce — he married it.

His jealous girlfriend, Jackie Taylor, had warned him: "It's the vegetable or me," after Steve spent long evenings on the allotment caring for the plant.

But jilted Jackie's jaw dropped in amazement when Steve stormed: "I'll take the lettuce. Her name's Laura and we'll wed in the Spring"

And they did just that last week, we can exclusively reveal.

In an astonishing ceremony which shocked his family, lovestruck Steve, 19, and his wacky vegetable said "I do."

The amazing marriage stunned passers-by at the Newcastle cabbage patch as wedding guests took their place among rows of beans and bunches of carrots.

But for dark-haired Steve, the magic moment was when his prize bloom, glowing with health from a diet of fresh water and Baby Bio, turned her head towards him for start of the blessing.

As the makeshift minister called for silence and began the bizarre service with lettuce pray, the outdoor congregation held its breath.

Smitten Steve, sporting a natty orange flower — no relation — pledged to love, honour and never dish up his tasty bride as a Waldorf Salad.

Green-headed Laura wore just a dash of sauce to ensure she was the best-dressed lettuce in Newcastle, a wedding guest revealed.

LETTUCE PRAY . . . the ceremony

Gone off the rails

RAILWAY guards are being phased out in favour of one-man operation. But the changeover has become a farce.

A guard told me the older workers at his depot are not being given redundancy. Instead they report for work and are then sent home because they're not needed.

And they often get called in on Sundays — at overtime rates!

MARILYN MONROE FOUND WORKING AS A STRIPPER

We unwrap yet another steamy showbiz exclusive

Silver screen goddess Marilyn Monroe is back from the dead – and is working as an erotic dancer in a seedy strip joint.

The pouting sexpot giggles as she wiggles her 38-inch boobs in front of drunken, wolf-whistling punters in the country's most notorious nightspots, Sunday Sport can exclusively reveal.

Lusty locals drool into their pint-pots watching the world's most famous film idol perform her sleazy act with four busty, bondage-clad beauties.

"It is just the sort of dirty dance that sends the men crazy," says the movie megastar. But the drinkers who flock to lear at Marilyn's sexy curves don't realise the dancer on stage is Caroline Taylor... the movie-star reincarnated.

British UFO experts stunned as . . .

PET-FANCYING ALIENS BEAM UP 26 ELEPHANTS

YOU'LL GET CAUGHT IN THE STAMPEDE TO READ THIS STORY

EXPERTS were last night reeling at reports of how aliens beamed up 26 elephants from a safari park.

Stunned eyewitnesses say the jumbos were sucked up by a silver "Tardis" which hovered over their heads.

And the entire event — which happened in broad daylight — has been hailed as a life-saving gesture by friendly alien visitors.

"When I first heard about this I thought it was a staged-managed event. But after investigating the sighting I'm convinced it did happen," said UFO investigation Rex Dutta, from Camberley, Surrey.

Rex — director of UFO magazine Viewpoint Aquarius — had the sighting checked out by one his crack investigators, Jose Lazare, in Spain.

Jose's report said the spaceship was silver and shaped like an upturned bowl.

The 250-foot silver spaceship shot down a beam of purple light which lifted the beasts into its hold.

"The craft hovered over the elephants. Suddenly they were bathed in purple light and lifted into the ship. The whole episode lasted for about two minutes," said Rex.

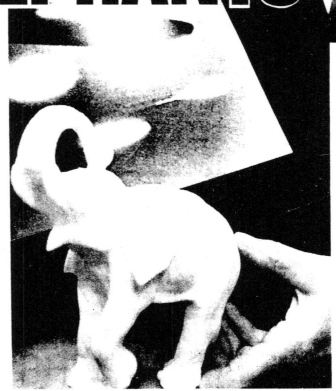

CONVINCED ... UFO expert Rex Dutta investigating the reports

PAMPERED PETS

DOGS with more than just a little puppy fat are being booked into a special canine health farm in Colorado.

They go walkies at least four times a day, have supervised swims and a strict diet of just half a cup of doggie dinner.

I SWALLOWED A SPIDER

IT WRIGGLED AND JIGGLED AND TICKLED INSIDE (and perhaps I'll die)

By BILL CORKE

STARVING teenager Andrew Campbell was forced to eat killer SPIDERS when he got lost in a snow-bound forest.

The freezing youngster, who hadn't eaten for three days, RIPPED the legs off deadly TARANTULAS before gobbling them whole.

The nightmare started for Andrew, 15, when he became hopelessly lost on a fishing trip and crawled into a hollow tree trunk to shelter from the cold.

"I hadn't eaten for three days when, all of a sudden, I felt something crawling across my face," the teenager recalled.

"The next think I knew, my whole body was a writhing mass of spiders. They were in my hair, on my back and stomach and even down my underpants.

"I was delirious with hunger and the first thing to come into my mind was to start eating them," he said.

Tarantula

Amazingly, Andrew wasn't bitten ONCE during his terrifying ordeal in the vast 200,000-acre Cleveland National Forest, California.

A tarantula bite can kill a victim in less than 30 minutes!

The boy's troubles started when he lost his way in the snow-covered forest and walked deeper and deeper into the dense undergrowth.

Crawling

"Because the conditions were so cold, there was nothing to eat. Everytning was covered with snow," said Andrew, of Guatay, California.

"After three days I was so weak, I was crawling on my hands and knees looking for shelter, when I found the tree stump."

Twenty four hours after his beastly feast, Andrew staggered to a highway where a passing motorist picked him up and drove him to hospital.

Frostbite

At California's San Diego Hospital, Dr Alan Horowitch said: "Andrew was suffering from severe blood poisoning when he was admitted.

STARVING... Andrew

"We had to remove the tips of his toes because of frostbite, but our chief concern was about the poisoning.

"He suffered at least three strokes as a result of his ordeal. It's lucky he's alive.

"Andrew is a very resourceful boy. In the same circumstances, I would probably have eaten the spiders too," the doctor added.

Nip and run dog

GOLDEN Labrador Klaus is in the doghouse for snatching women's purses.

The seven-year-old dog perfected the art of grabbing handbags and racing back to drop them at the feet of his owner Franz Bournhoff.

The 41-year-old unemployed computer technician told a court he trained Klaus in the snap-and-run technique because his ex-wife and three children were taking all his money.

Nabbed

But the purse-snatching dog's career came to an abrupt end when he was nabbed by another dog.

Police told a Munich court that Klaus grabbed the bag of a young woman outside a butcher's.

He pelted off to a nearby park where owner Franz was hiding.

But the woman had her alsatian with her. She unleashed the dog and it chased Klaus to the park and cornered Franz, who was later arrested.

Franz said he first trained Klauz to fetch purses just for fun, then later decided to make some money with the trick.

WORLD WAR 2 BOMBER

Amazing shock pictures inside today

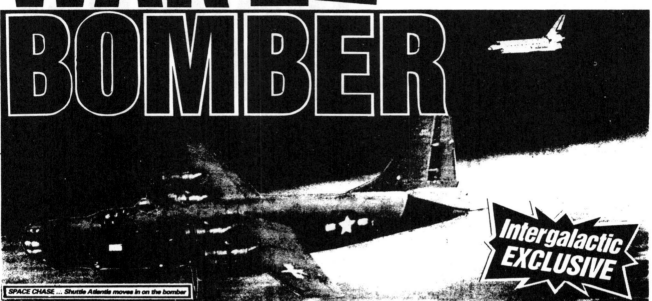

SPACE CHASE ... Shuttle Atlantis moves in on the bomber

Intergalactic EXCLUSIVE

FOUND IN SPACE

By JACK CANT, Cape Canaveral

FIVE astronauts have blasted into outer space on a top secret mission to capture the World War II bomber found on the Moon.

Headed by Captain 'Hoots'' Gibson, the NASA team took off in the Space Shuttle Atlantis on a classified mission this week.

But the news blackout is shattered today by these amazing satellite pictures of the shuttle in a space chase with the bomber 160 miles above the Earth.

US President tells Shuttle astronauts to tow home lost plane

NAFFED OFF HUBBY MARRIES GOAT

Grandad weds his nanny...

TOGETHER . . . man and beast

HEN-PECKED hubby Norbert Kuntsch got fed up with his wife's constant nagging—so he divorced her and married a GOAT!

Now the madcap millionaire has cut off his money-grabbing ex-wife without a penny and is leaving his entire fortune to his GOAT-BRIDE Becky.

Upholding his divorce claim—on grounds of mental cruelty—a court in Hamburg, West Germany, ruled that Norbert's marriage to the goat is perfectly LEGAL.

Grandad Norbert, 83, got to the end of his tether when ex-wife Doris, 31, began demanding more and more of his cash to pay for her expensive tastes.

"After five months of marriage she became a right COW. She was screaming and nagging at me day and night," said Norbert.

"From the first day we got married, Doris changed into a vicious animal and began spending my money like water."

Shock

But for long-suffering Norbert, the final straw came when he found an unmailed letter she had written to her secret LOVER.

Norbert's frail heart nearly stopped when he read: "I can't wait until the old goat dies and we'll be rich."

He stumbled out of his mansion in a state of shock and began walking around his estate to clear his head.

"I was just wondering how some one could be so BEASTLY when this beautiful white goat walked shyly over to me and licked my hand," Norbert recalled.

"The little animal had

By BILLY CORKE

strayed onto my land. She seemed so innocent . . . the exact OPPOSITE of my wife. Then I got an idea."

Norbert went to the farmer who owned four-year-old Becky and paid £50 for her, took her home and waited for his wife to return from one of her many shopping sprees.

"When she came in I told her I was divorcing her . . . and that there was someone else," said Norbert.

"At that moment Becky came trotting into the room with a little bell tinkling around her neck.

"Doris gasped at me in amazement and called me a dirty old pervert. But I just laughed at her and told her to get out and move on to new PASTURES."

Three months later, Norbert celebrated his divorce by immediately MARRYING Becky the goat.

An aged shepherd witnessed the touching common-law ceremony in a local turnip field.

"Of course I don't REALLY love Becky as a WIFE, I just did it to give Doris the send-off she deserved," Norbert said.

Outraged Doris, his second wife, fumed: "He's a DISGUSTING old man. I gave him the best five months of my life."

MUM GRABS GHOST BY THE GHOULIES

ECSTASY . . . Renee

See-through lover for OAP Renee

TREMBLING pensioner Renee Meyer told last night of her steamy nights of passion — with a superstud GHOST called Charlie!

And, with a smile on her face, the divorcee added: "I'm in heaven when he appears in my bed at night."

Mother-of-two Renee, who is 63, had been living alone in her council flat in Stoke Newington, north London, until Charlie turned up on Christmas Day SEVEN years ago.

"I was terrified at first," Renee told Sunday Sport, "but then we became friends. Very, very good friends!

"No man alive has ever

By JACK KRUGER

made me feel like Charlie does, when he comes to me.

"You don't know the things he does to me and the tricks we get up to. I am lucky if I get any sleep at all!

"I am totally submissive. He orders me to take off my clothes — and I do. I obey his every command and satisfy his every whim and fancy," she said.

"One night, just to see if I was really obedient, he told me to clean the flat.

"And, would you believe, I was on my hands and knees, at three in the morning, scrubbing my kitchen floor!"

Renee, who was born in Oran, Algeria, and came to Britain in the Sixties — she was divorced in 1974 — went on:

"I had a terrible time when I was married.

"My husband continually beat me up and the police were round here all the time.

"Now I have Charlie and my life has completely turned around. I am in ecstasy."

A former typist in a City tax office, Renee revealed how the ghost first turned up in her flat.

"I had just taken my Christmas turkey out of the oven. I don't have much money and I decided to treat myself that year," she recalled.

"But as soon as I started carving, there was a terrible smell in the room.

"Then strange things began happening and I could definitely feel a presence. I was no longer alone.

"I was terrified and didn't know what to do."

Then Charlie gave her a Christmas present — and has been around ever since.

RUDI'S COMEBACK!

HOUSEWIFE Wende Gross told last night how she shared her bed for FOUR years with the ghost of Hollywood stud Rudolph Valentino in the seaside home the star once owned.

"This is definitely the strangest place I've ever

By SIMON FINLAY

lived," said Wende, 44, who hired GHOSTBUSTERS Debbie and Richard Senate to flush Rudi out.

Medium Debbie told Wende: "I have a feeling of an extremely sexual man. He wants to make his presence known to you, when you are in bed."

Wende says that since he appeared at her home in Los Angeles, she's had "nothing but trouble". . . including her catching TB and her boyfriend dying.

Really sick parrot

HENRY the sex-mad parrot, has given his owners the bird and skipped his comfortable nest.

The foul-mouthed bird, whose favourite phrase is: "Do you drop 'em?", has girls blushing as he wolf whistles from the trees.

And his owner, Mrs. Marlene Guest, thinks the randy bird could be on the look out for a mate.

Henry, a green Amazon parrot, flew through an open window at Marlene's home in Rotherham, South Yorkshire, two weeks ago, and ever since has been feeding in a neighbour's fruit trees.

Marlene is now chasing round the neighbourhood in her car with sticks of celery and a set of step ladders in search of the loony bird.

She said: "People think I'm daft.

When I shout to him, Henry just says: "Hello darlin, do you drop 'em?," and wolf whistles."

WOMAN TRAPPED ON BUS FOR 30 YEARS

THIS clapped-out coach was the grim prison for a frail pensioner

EXCLUSIVE

A WEAK and bewildered granny was last night recovering in hospital after being trapped on a bus for THIRTY years.

Pathetic Hortencia del Vecchio, 63, emerged howling and sobbing from the Number 36 school bus, where she'd been TIED to a seat for three decades.

And as the frail pensioner staggered her first steps since she was 33 years old, her family confessed: "We're the ones who tied her up . . . but it was all for her own GOOD."

Brother Ernesto claimed Hortencia went raving MAD when her husband died in 1953.

"She would throw pots and pans, curse and go into mad rages — attacking me and my sister Isabel," said the farm worker.

"I didn't know what to do. My uncle told me the best thing was just to tie her up. So we roped her to a seat on the old school bus near our home."

During her horrific ordeal, crazy Hortencia was forced to sleep among rotten food and human waste on the broken-down old banger at Arroyo Seco, Argentina.

Passers by heard constant moaning and groaning through the bus door — but mistook the whimpering for a small dog or wild animal.

PRISONER . . . granny Hortencia

ONE-EYED MARS MONSTER THROWN FROM UFO

HORRIFIC . . . one-eyed space tot fell to Earth

HORRIFIED doctors caring for a monstrous one-eyed baby have told the world: "This tot came from Mars!"

They believe the galaxy's ugliest child was thrown out of a passing UFO by an alien mother who screamed: "Get this thing out of my sight!"

And medics say they can hardly blame her after seeing the bulbous frog-like baby, with one huge eye bursting out of its bonce.

Thick monkey hair covered its stomach and the creature had the strong hands and feet of a baboon.

Fears the monster was ejected from an inter-galactic playpen have been fuelled by reports of an object hurtling to earth just hours before the discovery.

"This unusual deformed newborn could well have come from outer space," admitted Dr Salvador Torres Garcia, in Mexico.

"For one thing it has an enormous eye set squarely on the top of its head. It looks more Martian than human.

"The nose, lips and cheeks have been compressed into a grotesque sort of face that is scary," he added, from City Police Headquarters in Mexico City.

The Martian monster was handed over to nurses at a Green Cross Clinic in the Baluena district of Mexico by two terrified farm workers.

"These two characters came in out of the cold, behaving very strangely. They had a package wrapped in newspapers," said staff intern, Carlos Sanchez.

"Hands visibly shaking, they opened the papers . . . and I got the shock of my life when I saw an eye staring sightlessly back at me."

At an autopsy crowded with curious doctors from all over Mexico, the monster baby was found to have TWO hearts, rudimentary lungs and a distorted internal tract.

In a hospital blunder, the men who brought in the monster were allowed to go home before their names were taken.

But Carlos Sanchez recalled their amazing report of the object falling out of the sky.

"One of them spoke of seeing something fall from the sky before they came across the body," he said.

"This is what gave credence to the rumours of a Martian monster thrown out of a spaceship."

Boy wonder

DOCTORS are up in arms over a tiny chain-smoking tot who works miracles. People in Rangoon flock to three-year-old "Dr Pon", who uses roots to cure all sorts of illnesses — for a handful of cigarettes.

GREMLINS ATE MY BABY

HORROR . . . as a little girl is eaten alive by grisly greedy Gremlins

HOUSEWIFE Kate Knorr told last night of her liquidizer battle with real-life Gremlins who GOBBLED up her daughter.

For fluffy chihuahua dog pups Kate bought as presents turned into flesh-devouring monsters overnight — just like in the

EXCLUSIVE

By JACK CANT, under a Christmas tree, Norway

Steven Spielberg blockbuster.

After they snaffled up her eight-year-old Susie, quick-thinking Kate fed them into a liquidizer . . . knowing it's the only way to stop a Gremlin eating.

And she revealed the two Christmas-present puppies only turned into Gremlins when she fed them AFTER midnight.

"That was the story in Gremlins, the movie," she sobbed last night.

"If the chihuahua-like creatures were fed late they turned into MONSTERS.

"It was the one rule of caring for them you must never break — if you did they turned into little demons.

"How could I know my own pet presents would behave in the same hideous and depraved manner?

"They ripped little Susie to pieces and then burped out her bones all over the house!"

The horror attack came when little Susie went downstairs for a late-night glass of milk.

A gruesome paw reached out from the kitchen dog basket where the Gremlins should have been sleeping and, within minutes, she was GOBBLED.

"It is one case of the truth being stranger than fiction," said local police chief Bjorn Dolder.

Clutching Susie's blue hair ribbon to her heaving bosom, Kate Knorr wept as she revealed the real-life Gremlins transformation.

For, just like in the smash-hit movie screened on Thursday:

● The pet shop owner WARNED Kate not to feed her little dogs after midnight;

CHRISTMAS blockbuster Gremlins features cute little creatures called Mogwai — that mustn't be fed after midnight.

Then their owner Billy Paltzer (played by Zach Galligan) gives in to the Mogwai's plea for food, they turn into razor-toothed monsters.

Watch out for the movie that turned into a real-life Gremlin horror when it's shown on ITV on Thursday, at 9pm.

● After dinner they sprouted BAT-LIKE ears and RAZOR teeth;

● They only died when she fed their evil bodies through a liquidizer.

Standing in her Gremlin-splattered kitchen near Sorfold, Kate, 39, showed me how she ended her nightmare . . .

"I jammed one in the liquidizer and its head flew off and exploded against the wall," she said.

"Then I shut the other in the microwave until it went POP! It was the only thing these swine understood.

"But all I want is my daughter back — and I know that can never be."

Husband Randi had this message for the world: "Chihuahua owners beware. Feed these dogs with the greatest of care . . . or YOUR daughter could be next."

SHORT CUT

A DESPERATE doctor cut himself open and took his own appendix out while stranded in a six-mile traffic jam.

Stunned drivers saw him take his surgical bag from the back seat and bite his leather belt to ease the agony before operating.

A woman took one look at blood spurting from his side and collapsed.

"That's when I ordered everyone back into their cars," said Dr Ira Khan, 35.

"What I didn't need at that point was a bunch of spectators."

Dr. Khan coolly drove himself to hospital in Beirut, Lebanon.

WORLD'S OLDEST WOMAN GOES BONKING MAD

'She wears frills — and sexy pink knickers'

SEX-CRAZY... that's tobacco-chewing Carrie at 114

THE oldest woman in the world went bonking mad last night... after being freed from a loony-bin.

Randy wrinkly Carrie White last had her leg over in 1909 — the year Henry Ford began producing his Model T car.

By JOHN GARVEY

But despite being 114 years old and barely able to walk, she is still crazy for NOOKIE.

So, in a desperate attempt to pull the fellas, Carrie wears make-up, posh hats, frilly dresses... and sexy pink UNDERWEAR.

Just one thing, though, puts the guys off...

The potty pensioner insists on chewing evil-smelling tobacco.

And then spitting out the horrible green goo as she PUCKERS up her lips for a kiss.

Poor Carrie's hubby had her committed to the nuthouse 80 years ago.

He told doctors she had gone BONKERS after developing post-typhoid psychosis.

Carrie had been alone and forgotten in the mental asylum in America's sunshine state of Florida ever since.

But now amazed experts have discovered she was never mad at all.

Her evil husband had just wanted to get shot of her.

Padded

This week Carrie was moved from her padded cell to a nearby old folk's home.

And she STUNNED nurses there with her desperate search for a man.

Matron Marjories Allen said: "Carrie brushes her hair, wears jewellery and primps herself up.

"Then she gazes at her image in the mirror and goes all flirty, making lovey-dovey cooing noises.

"We've tried to persuade her to use chewing gum instead," said Mrs Allen. "But she won't have it."

Researchers for the Guinness Book of Records have confirmed that Carrie is the oldest person in the world. They plan to include her in their next edition.

HERE'S what was happening when Carrie last got her leg over:

Henry Asquith was Prime Minister and Edward the Seventh was on the throne.

Old Age Pensions were introduced by Lloyd George, then Chancellor of the Exchequer, later to be Prime Minister himself.

Also in 1909, Bleriot made his first flight across the English Channel and Henry Ford began producing his Model T car classic.

China's cuddle crisis

LOVESICK Chinese are turning to Western ways to help them find Comrade Right.

Peking now has its own computer dating agency.

But it just can't cope with the masses of lonely hearts looking for romance.

So more than 100 men and women of all ages stand around sheepishly in the grounds of the Workers' Cultural Palace every Sunday afternoon, hoping to find a mate.

But they've not been as lucky as the microchip marvel — 200 of the couples it matched up this year have already got married.

Dotty dictator's life as a woman
EVIL JAP EMPEROR SPEAKS FROM HEAVEN

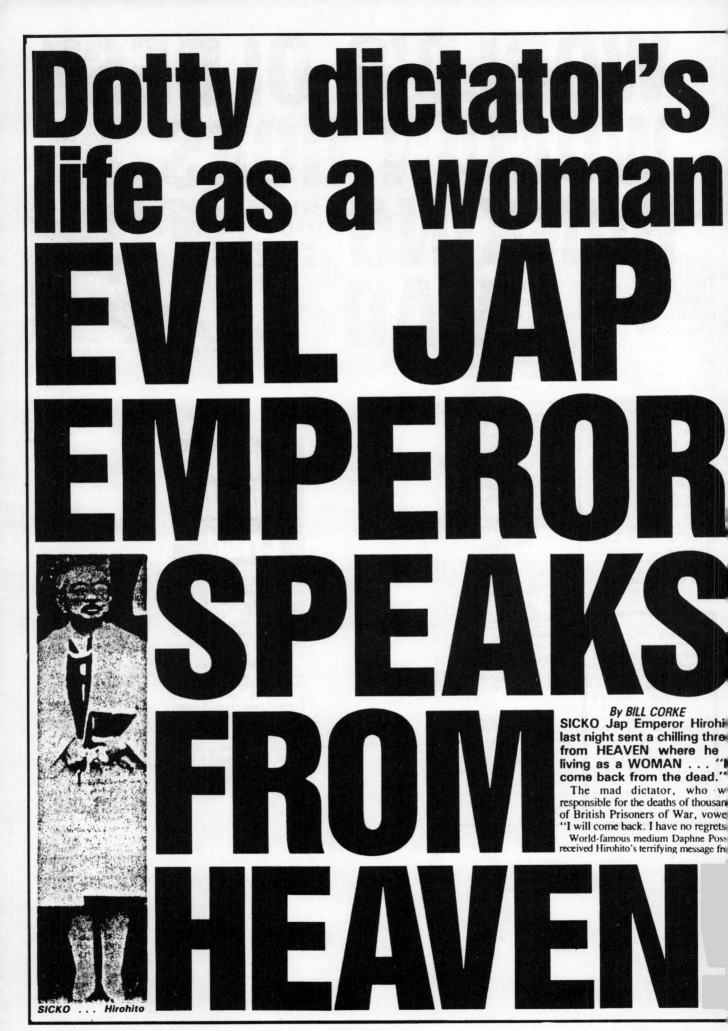

SICKO . . . Hirohito

By BILL CORKE

SICKO Jap Emperor Hirohi[
last night sent a chilling thre[
from HEAVEN where he [
living as a WOMAN . . . "[
come back from the dead."[

The mad dictator, who w[
responsible for the deaths of thousan[
of British Prisoners of War, vowe[
"I will come back. I have no regrets.[

World-famous medium Daphne Poss[
received Hirohito's terrifying message fr[

ALIEN BABY FOUND IN JUNGLE

Space-age tot living with family of apes

A TARZAN space baby has been found deep in the Amazon jungle — raised by gorillas as a chest-thumping Lord of the Apes.

The alien tot with pointy Mr Spock ears has been hailed as Tarzan 2001 by boffins who found it in the arms of mother monkeys.

With a single nostril in the middle of its button nose and spooky mirror eyes, it is believed a careless alien mum let it fall out of a UFO pram.

But space-watchers have warned it could be the first of an alien invasion force reared to conquer Earth like Tarzan tamed the jungle.

"This is the scientific find of the century," Dr Burton Spiller told natives in the Amazon basin village of Anori, according to reporters.

"The child is living proof that intelligent life exists somewhere other than Earth.

"For reasons we don't understand someone has delivered him to us — although it could have litterally fallen to Earth."

Monkey

Believed to be just 16 months old, the space baby was found by a group of athropologists who at first thought it was a retarded human child.

Surrounded by a family of gorillas, the tot squarked in an alien version of ape language and grubbed on the ground like a monkey.

But having saved the space child from its monkey minders the scientists became convinced it was of a much higher intelligence.

"The child is strong for his age," said Dr Spiller —

By JACK CANT
Up the Amazon 2am this morning

confirming fears the baby was being brought up as Lord of the Apes by the muscle-bound gorillas.

"The baby is under observation around the clock by scientists and we are learning more about him every day," added the Swiss scientist.

"He speaks fluently, but in a language that we have not yet been able to understand.

"We are most interested in his eyes. Sometimes, they become mirror-like — you can actually see your face in them."

Conquerors

Meanwhile, local UFO-watchers have given out a warning that the Tarzan alien might be a spy for an invading army.

"Dr Spiller talks about the baby as if it were a gift to humanity from another world, but it could as easily be a SCOURGE," said Amazonian UFO researcher, Tajano de Morais.

Foolish

"I think it's foolish to take a chance. He might even be a spy among us or a scout for a race of alien conquerors," he added.

But keeping the extraordinary tot under wraps in a secret jungle hideaway, Dr Spiller said the alien must be considered friendly until proved otherwise.

BINMAN TURNS INTO DOG

Fun for Fido

...and he's having a barking great time

FORMER binman Peter Long made a sensational confession last night: "I have turned into a DOG."

His shocked family watched as he SPROUTED a furry coat, GREW canine fangs and began PANTING after bitches.

Now Peter's wife, June, and his two children have disowned him completely after his canine capers left him in the doghouse.

"IT all began two years ago when I met Barbara Woodhouse in the butchers," barked Peter from his kennel in New Road, Rickmansworth, Herts.

BEFORE...dustman Peter.

"She called me to heel right there and then and I have never been the same since.

"I began feeling a bit wuff and I staggered outside and found myself transforming into a mongrel."

Now he gets called PAL—short for Peter Arthur Long—or Rover by his human friends at his local, the Fox and Hounds.

They make sure he doesn't lead a dog's life by putting brandy in his dog bowl, and taking him to the park.

"I'm used to being a dog now and I love the life," said Peter.

"It was a bit hard at first and my family just couldn't understand it, but now I never want to go back to being human again."

Name game

YOUR name could be a big turn-on say American experts.

For a woman's name has a lot to do with attracting men.

Top of a poll of male students was Christine, which was most associated with purity and beauty.

Also high on the list were Anne, Lisa, Kim and Mary.

Names voted a big no-no were Florence, Mildred, Myrtle, Ehtel and Edna.

But the study led by a professor at New York State University also revealed the girls with less attractive names were likely to get better jobs because they were considered to have brains rather than beauty.

PENSIONER CHOKED BY KILLER SPROUT

STAFF at a club for the partially blind thought pensioner John Wheeler was waving because he wanted to go to the toilet . . . but really he was CHOKING to death.

For, tragically, the frail 60-year-old was fighting for breath after getting a Brussels sprout stuck in his throat.

And while retired Surrey roadworker John desperately waved his arm in the air, rescuers tried to carry him to the loo . . . but he collapsed and DIED.

"His false teeth did not fit and he couldn't chew very well," John's tearful widow, Winifred, told a hushed inquest.

Tragic

"But he didn't want to draw attention to the fact that he needed his food to be cut up for him," she added.

Grief-stricken Winifred,

By GAZZA THOMPSON

of St Paulsgate, Wokingham, said her husband needed all his food to be chopped into small pieces since suffering two strokes.

He had sometimes put food into his mouth and forgotten to swallow it, she revealed.

When tragic John had begun choking in the past, she would push on his stomach to try and dislodge it with a sudden rush of air.

But even though the pensioner had been attending a partially-sighted club at a Reading community centre for more than two years, staff said they were not aware he had difficulty swallowing.

Attention

The centre's organiser, Jean Urquhart, spoke of how John died as he tucked in to his Christmas dinner last month.

She admitted a woman told her the pensioner was in need of attention, but when she reached his table John did not speak to her.

She and a helper tried to lead him towards the loo after John pointed in that direction – but the old man collapsed back into his chair and died.

Choking

Consultant pathologist Dr Robert Williams later revealed that John had died from choking on the killer sprout.

He confirmed that other items of food the pensioner had swallowed had also not been chewed.

Coroner Dr Joe Pym recorded a verdict of accidental death at this week's inquest.

False teeth for miracle dog

AN 11-month-old pup has astonished vets by her miraculous escape after a 70ft. plunge on to concrete.

But now "Blue" desperately needs doggie dentures to replace her lost teeth.

While her mouth heals the mongrel has to eat scrambled eggs — at a rate of 80 a week.

Owner Chris Ward, of Canford Heath, Bournemouth, said: "It's quite expensive. We're just glad she's alive."

Blue had bounded through the window of a fourth floor flat. Vets said she probably passed out with fear, making her limp and less likely to break any bones.

"The fall would have killed the average human," added Mr. Ward.

MY DAD IS GOOD ON BUSTS

By MADELEINE PALLAS

YOU could have heard a pin drop. And the assembled politicians, peers and foreign VIPs were waiting to see what would happen next.

Suddenly Prince Charles, who was about to unveil a plaque, broke the silence: "I really don't know why I am doing this at all," he told them with a wry grin . . .

"Papa's far more used to unveiling busts than I am!"

It was a joke. But according to ex-Royal butler, Billy Barry, Prince Charles knew his father's reputation as a man with an eye for a pretty face.

"The Duke of Edinburgh had a real reputation as a ladies' man," said Billy.

Watcher

"Among his own circles he was referred to as a watcher of the fillies."

The incident happened at the exclusive opening of the Duke of Edinburgh lounge in the Royal Thames Yacht Club, where Billy was serving drinks.

"But no-one batted an eyelid. They'd all been knocking back the vintage port and were laughing," says Billy.

Charles' rude jibe at Philip

"But there are plenty of people who could tell some juicy stories about Prince Philip's wild youth."

It was just one of the revealing episodes that Billy, 31, saw over several years as a fly-on-the-wall observer in the Royals' homes.

Billy is a cousin of Stephen Barry, Prince Charles' gay valet who died of AIDs last year. But although Stephen had betrayed the Royals by writing his memoirs for £1 million, Billy was trusted.

Billy, who became a familiar face at Buckingham Palace, spoke of other occasions when the Queen's husband made his appreciation of beautiful girls obvious.

"Prince Philip was blatently proud of the fact that his son Prince Andrew had lots of girlfriends," said Billy.

"He was always talking of the pretty young things that Andrew kept bringing around."

FUN

MIKE Atkelsky is keeping his donkey Sally warm in Hampshire's New Forest with leg warmers held up by suspenders borrowed from his wife.

SPOT

After travelling through tunnel of light...
SPACECRAFT TAKES PHOTOS OF HEAVEN

Amazing shots inside today

SCENES MATCH DESCRIPTION OF LIFE-AFTER-DEATH

RUNCIE . . . Interested

INCREDIBLE space pictures of HEAVEN were last night backed by the Vatican as GENUINE.

As Church of England boss Robert Runcie pledged to look into the sensational snaps of Paradise, allegedly taken by a space probe, the Pope's advisors agreed they had to be possible proof of an after life.

"There must be something in them," confessed Pope John Paul's personal spokesman on supernatural matters, Father Andreas Resch.

EXCLUSIVE

"We promise to analyse the pictures and give a proper explanation — we must consider the camera never lies."

The pictures show a spectacular gateway into Heaven taken by a Soviet satellite then smuggled out of the country and into the West.

They later appeared in America, backed by the sensational claims.

Sensational

Sunday Sport investigators were handed copies of the first ever views of the Pearly Gates and then passed them on to Lambeth Palace.

Now Britain's spiritual leader Dr Robert Runcie has pledged a top level probe into the amazing scenes which have sent church leaders into an almighty flap.

The amazing pictures have been dubbed "the most fantastic Christian find since the Turin shroud."

While churchmen from London and Rome study the astonishing evidence that Heaven is left of the planet Pluto, shocked Russian defence chiefs, who snapped them, are desperately ducking questions.

The Ruskies would only admit it was their galactic spy in the sky which beamed back fantastic pictures of the Hereafter.

GREENFLY ATE MY LOVER!

Heartless insects put end to mixed-salad marriage

SHATTERED . . . Steve and Laura and (below) flashback to last week.

HEARTBROKEN gardener Steve Mahon was being comforted by relatives last night after a swarm of killer greenfly ate his lettuce lover.

The ruthless attack on Laura's lush leaves came after Steve left her to soak up some sun on the patio of their modest terrace home.

Newcastle's oddball couple hit the headlines last week when we exclusively revealed she was the first fruity salad to marry a human.

But just six days after they wed — she was dead.

Neighbours claim a mass of mean greenfly, which had already devastated their potted plants, savaged Laura the lettuce, leaving just her bare stalk.

"It was just like something out of a horror film," said close chum Jim Smith.

"Steve had doused her with insect repellent, but it didn't make any difference.

"They just made a beeline for her, and within seconds had munched their way through her outer leaves."

Laura's mixed marriage was hailed as a first for the vegetable world after lovesick Steve ditched his long-term girlfriend to say "I do" to Laura.

By RUKI SAYID

Jilted lover Jackie Taylor vowed to turn Laura into a Waldorf Salad if she ever got her hands on her.

But yesterday, Jackie, 18, admitted she still loved Steve.

"I'll have him back if he's willing to turn over a new leaf," she said.

"But he's got to promise to give up gardening. I couldn't bear to lose him to a carrot or pea-pod."

Shattered Steve was too distraught to talk about his short-lived marriage.

Friends say he just sits indoors watching Gardener's World over and over again.

"He's trying to recapture the magic he had with Laura," revealed Jim, 19.

"But he's got to realise that if anyone could have saved Laura, she would be a vegetable now. The greenfly didn't leave much."

Steve is planning to bury her stalk in the vegetable patch where he first fell for her leafy charms.

FIRED

AN arrow which went wide of the mark sparked off a riot in an African village.

Two brothers were slugging it out when one lost his temper, grabbed his bow and arrow and let fly.

But the arrow struck down an innocent bystander whose enraged relatives set light to the killer's home.

The fire spread engulfing 17 neighbouring grass huts in the Kenyan village.

DOC MAKES AN ONION WEEP

CRACKPOT doc Dieter Hoffman has vowed never to eat vegetables again . . . after he cut into an onion and heard it SCREAM.

"It was crying out for mercy. It was as if I'd cut a human or animal to the bone," sobbed dotty Dieter, a top psychic researcher in West Germany.

"Now I'm only eating dairy products. At least cheese feels no pain."

ZOMBIE ZAP! WARS

A SOVIET plot to enslave the West by turning us into mindless zombies has been unmasked.

For evil Russian scientists have invented a laser zap gun which can cook the brain.

The fearsome, Star Trek-style weapon — more lethal and selective than the neutron bomb — can also EXPLODE the enemy from hundreds of miles away.

But a leading NATO scientist has warned that scheming Soviet boffins have a more sinister plot in mind . . .

Jonathan Tennenbaum revealed: "Russian theorists have worked out that it's wasteful to zap men, women and children to death instead they can burn their brains into vegetable existences, useful as slave labour."

The weapon works like a microwave oven and can literally cook a man, intelligence sources say.

Western military strategists believe the Soviets are way ahead of them in the microwave laser technology and are desperately trying to catch up.

Experts believe the edge the Russians have can explain their readiness to

By JAN HARDY

agree to nuclear war-head reductions.

The Soviets are already operating death ray weapon systems which range from laser pistols to gigantic dishes which can operate from space stations or even the moon.

They can be used to blast selected targets on earth or other satellites in space.

Although the theorists are dreaming about turning us all into the walking dead, obeying their very command, the generals are more interested in being able to strike quickly during a full-scale war.

Mr Tennenbaum, director of the European Fusion Energy Foundation in Wiesbaden, West Germany, says the microwave

laser beams can "knock out the brain, nervous system and other organs within range . . . quite literally they would be microwaved to death."

He added: "The Russian generals are planning to use these weapons in initial sorties by Spetznas commando squads behind enemy lines in the event of a Third World War.

"The plan is to knock out Britain and NATO command centres and key bases minutes after an all out strike by Warsaw Pact forces.

"The principle is frighteningly simple. If the brains of a few thousand NATO personnel are destroyed a few minutes before warning of a Warsaw Pact attack, then armed defence would practically cease to exist."

Cortina makes big splash

TRAWLERMEN reckoned there was something fishy going on when a Ford Cortina headed towards them . . . in the middle of the Irish Sea.

When they looked closely they saw there was no driver behind the wheel.

They alerted the Isle Of Man coastguard who found it was a floating target that broke its moorings during stormy weather a hundred miles away in Wales.

The white Cortina shell had been welded onto a

floating pontoon and is one of many used for shooting practice by the Navy.

It took two days to cross the Irish Sea. A Royal Navy frigate was called in and blew up the old banger four miles off the Isle of Man coast.

"We find many unusual things floating in the sea but this is the first time we've had a car and especially one that's travelled so far".

BOY, 13 EATS MUM

A RAVENOUS schoolboy turned cannibal in an incredible hunger binge – he carved up his mum and dad and ate them for tea.

In a Mother's Day shocker, evil Carl Sontoya turned his parents into a bubbling stew and tucked in, it is claimed.

Horrified neighbours of the 13-year-old monster say they saw his parents' bones boiling in a pot on the family stove.

Grisly

Nextdoor neighbours stumbled on the grisly horror scene when they became suspicious after the couple disappeared.

"I was sickened by what I saw. There were large human bones in a pot on the stove," said neighbour Hernando Sedone.

"Young Carl was sitting in the living room. There was a look of evil on his face.

"But when I asked him, he wouldn't tell me where his parents were."

Astonished police who searched the house and garden couldn't find the bones or ANY trace of the missing couple.

And last night the teenager was still keeping mum about their disappearance.

A police spokesman said: "The boy refuses to talk. We do not know what to think.

Neighbour Hernando claims he also heard some sort of chilling ceremony taking place in the run-down house.

"Late at night, their house was dark except for candles, and you could hear chanting," he said.

AND DAD

BUDDY HOLLY FOUND ALIVE ...AS PEGGY SUE

EXCLUSIVE

FOUR-EYED singing legend Buddy Holly has made a beyond-the-grave comeback as a WOMAN called Peggy Sue.

Long dead Buddy, famed for tunes such as That'll Be The Day and Peggy Sue, turned up at a Texas bar this week in a pink frock.

The star, who was killed in a plane crash 30 years ago this Friday, flounced onto stage still wearing his trademark horn-rim glasses.

"Just call me, Peggy, ya'll," drawled the boy-turned-girl from the cowboy town of Lubbock, Texas.

Then the golden oldie ghostie launched into a high-pitched version of his classic number, Peggy Sue.

"I wrote this about a girlie nearly 35 years ago," he told astonished drinkers in the Cattle Ranch Bar outside wind-swept Lubbock.

"Then I realised it was all about me. Sometimes a man can be trapped in the wrong body."

Accompanying himself on a battered electric guitar, the ghost of the late Buddy Holly then did three more

By JACK CANT in Lubbock, Texas

numbers.

"I seen Buddy Holly play when I was a kid round these parts," said drinker Doug Kohler. "And it was the same guy.

"He was always a big awkward-looking feller with buck teeth . . . and thirty years on the other side hasn't changed him none.

"Only he was wearing that damn silly dress, of course, and walking like a fairy."

Other regulars were less tolerant — throwing beer cans and ashtrays at the tiny stage normally used by strippers.

"I always knew the Holly-boy was a god-damn pervert," snarled mechanic Brad Yuth.

"If I could get him on a plane again, I'd SHOOT the cotton-pickin' thing out of the air myself."

Landlady Alma Montgomery scoffed: "Some of the guys had a few too many. It didn't look

like Buddy to me. And I've never seen a corpse sing doo-wop."

Country boy Buddy was the world's number one popstar along with Elvis Presley.

After a string of hits with his band the Crickets, Buddy went on a US tour with La Bamba star Richie Valens and the Big Bopper.

All three were killed on February 3, 1959 when their plane crashed during a snowstorm.

■ **BROWN-EYED** handsome man, sang Buddy Holly when he led the chirping Crickets.

Now, say hard-drinking regulars at a Texas bar, he's back as a brown-eyed handsome woman.

For Buddy has come Slippin' and Slidin' back from the other side.

Here's how Buddy looked, according to those tall tale-telling Texans.

KILLER PLANTS STALK QUEEN MUM

Freak of nature puts royal in deadly danger

THE Queen Mum has been put at risk by a deadly plague of mutant shrubs.

A Triffid-like strain of the humble rhododendron is taking over her favourite gardens in killer clumps up to 20ft high.

And just one royal sniff of the scented shrub could send the 87-year-old great-grandma tumbling into her herbacious borders.

Armies of the shrubs, caused by a freak of nature, are towering above her favourite plot at Windsor Castle.

By JACK CANT

The deceptively beautiful purple bloom of the Ponticum strain has found its evil way into the gardens the Queen Mum planned and built with her late husband King George VI.

"They spread like wildlife, like something out of a horror movie," said Forestry Commission spokesman Steve O'Neill.

Deadly

"They kill anything that comes into their path," said the boffin, who does not know about the danger to the Queen Mum.

The problem has also struck at Exmoor National Park, where emergency teams of workmen have been sent to tackle the deadly shrub.

"It's been getting worse and it's not just in national parks, it's also found in Stately home gardens," said conservation manager Jeff Haynes.

"It is poisonous to mammals, birds and insects, and when it takes hold, everything else dies.

DANGER . . . Queen Mum

"We are extremely concerned — the plant has run riot."

The green-fingered royal has yet to be warned about the killer plant which has ravaged an area the size of Coventry in the last year.

Warned

"Yes, we've seen the Ponticum at Windsor. But we had no idea it was so dangerous," said a concerned royal workman.

The Queen Mum is expected to make her annual visit to the Chelsea Flower show tomorrow.

But one of the show's organisers warned: "There will be masses of rhododendrons at the exhibition."

Bride says 'I wool'

BRIDE Angela Rodulson had a cake to remember at her wedding — knitted by her mum.

Housewife Sylvia Rodulson explained: "I've knitted jumpers for all the family before, and prided myself on being able to knit anything.

"So I knitted the three-tier wedding cake!"

Sylvia, of Westwood, Peterborough, made a cardboard framework for the cake before knitting the covers, and then decorated it with lace and flowers.

She said: "It took three weeks to knit. I've never done anything like this before."

But some of the quests got the needle, because they couldn't eat it.

DIRTY

A COLLEGE survey says most women leave the loo without washing their hands.

Spies concealed in public toilets reported only three women out of 20 use a washbasin if they think they are alone.

But put an observer on the spot and 18 out of 20 will turn on the tap.

GHOST TAUNTS HIGH SPIRITS BOOZER

Steve meets on-set spook

We bust another ghostly exclusive

COMEDY star Steve Guttenberg was terrorised by a real-life spook on the set of the new ghost movie blockbuster High Spirits.

The spooky spectre materialised before the astonished actor as he relaxed with a bottle of Irish whiskey while making the film which opens this week.

But when Police Academy star Steve tried to banish the eerie apparition by leaving the haunted castle filmset and kicking the bottle . . . it followed him to Britain.

Heart-throb Steve first saw the hazy green man flying towards him in derelict Dromoland Castle, Limerick.

"He was really spooked," confided his agent, John Basteek. "Especially when he saw the same thing three days later.

"He was sitting in an old bedroom when he noticed a greenish blob which looked like a huge man floating around

By RAY LEVINE

above him on the ceiling."

Steve thought he'd escaped the ghost when he arrived in Britain to finish shooting with co-star Peter O'Toole at Shepperton Studios.

But the frightening fiend appeared again on a replica set of the castle.

Terrified Steve last night admitted that he had seen ghosts on the set.

"I absolutely believe in ghosts," said Steve. "After being in Limerick I saw two ghosts."

But the American star confessed the first spirit appeared after he'd been boozing on home-made hooch.

"It was after a couple of Irish moonshines — it's home-made whiskey. I'm not a specialist but I am quite partial," he said.

But Dromoland Castle IS haunted for real by ghosts of criminals who perished in its infamous dungeons.

"There are many legends surrounding the castle," said Yvonne O'Flaherty, who works at a nearby hotel in Limerick. "I wouldn't be at all surprised if he saw something."

Pull the other one . .

A MAN had to call an ambulance after getting a plastic ring stuck on a vital part of his anatomy in a sex session.

"The ring was stuck so fast he just couldn't remove it," said a spokesman.

Pain

"He was in some pain because he was tugging and pulling to get it off.

"Obviously it was a bit embarrassing because he wasn't alone in the house".

The Sunday Sport doctor said: "If he'd stopped tugging, the size of the problem would soon have been reduced."

MUM GIVES BIRTH TO AN 8lb TROUT!

EXCLUSIVE By RUKI SAYID

A YOUNG mum, who reckons she was bonked by a fish-faced alien, is terrified she will give birth to a healthy trout.

Doctors have already confirmed her scaly lover's child has gills behind its ears, a pouting mouth and two hearts.

Stunned medics, who were shocked by scans of the pregnant woman, revealed her outer space baby looks more like a baby trout swimming around her womb than a human foetus with arms and legs.

Now they're not sure whether it will need an aquarium or a cot when it's born in July.

"It's totally unlike anything I have ever seen," said top doctor Rolf Ahlqvist.

"The baby is half human and half extra-terrestrial. It's frightening and incredible — but true."

UFO experts believe the 32-year old woman was seduced by a slimy spaceman when randy trouts from outer space landed in Sweden in November.

Leading European researcher Jan van der Hoer revealed that ET watchers logged a sudden surge in alien activity near the unnamed mum-to-be's home around the time she concieved.

"It is possible that she was somehow rendered unconscious by the alien father and impregnated at that time," added Dr Ahlqvist.

The stunned woman, who is carrying the half-fish, half-Swode, already has two normal children and is married to a computer engineer.

Nuts about their baby

TWO rare monkeys have become proud parents... after their diet of nuts was changed.

They gave birth to an inch-long marmoset after three barren years in a cage at a pet shop in Borrowash, near Derby.

Owner Stuart Wakefield said: "It must have been something in their new brand of nuts."

Snap decision!

● HEADMASTER Alan Bevan has turned pooper snooper in a bid to stop dogs fouling the pavements outside his school. He stands guard with a camera at the gates every morning waiting to snap the messy mutts in the act.

Rita Dyer, deputy hed at the Cwm-Nedd Welsh School, West Glamorgan, said: "It's been a terrible problem for some time, but last week was the final straw, and Mr Bevan decided to take action. It's certainly worked, because since we let it be known we were keeping watch, the problem seems to have stopped."

If Mr Bevan snaps any canine culprits, he plans to hand the evidence to the local police.

PEEPING TOM ALIENS SPY ON OUR SEX ROMPS

BEARING UP UNDER STRAIN

A CAMERA-SHY bear who objected to a pilot taking sneaky aerial shots brought his plane down.

The big brown bear, which was fishing for salmon, got in a grisly mood when a low-flying observation plane dived down for a close-up.

It reared up and took a swipe at the plane damaging it enough to force an emergency landing at a nearby airport in Yakutat, Alaska.

SCARED . . . David

Dirty ETs love peek

By RAY LEVINE

RED-FACED hairdresser David Kirkham is being driven out of his house by Peeping Toms from outer-space!

Sex-pest spacemen have been getting an ET eyeful of David and his pretty wife Alison by hovering outside their bedroom window for a sneaky PEEK.

And now the embarrassed couple have shelved their sex-life in a bid to escape the slitty-eyed aliens, who bob up and down at the sight of anything SAUCY.

"It's ruining my sex life. I used to be a bit of a Tarzan, but now I'm too scared to undress unless the curtains are drawn and the lights are off," revealed worried David.

The 7ft tall spacemen squint through cracks in the curtains every time David gets up to hanky-panky with attractive Alison.

"I'm seriously thinking about moving house. I've complained to the council and the police, but they can't do ANYTHING," sighed the irate 36-year-old.

Another intergalactic exclusive...

CITY FOUND ON MARS

Aliens build giant phone

Your titbits

■ MY WIFE sat on the photo-copier at work and came home with a enormous copy of her naked bum.

While I've no objections to anything she gets up to at work, I wonder whether it will affect her ability to have children?　　　　*T.W. Teeside*

FIONA: *It shouldn't. But if you are THAT freewheeling about what she gets up to, make sure YOU are the father.*

─────────────

■ MY boyfriend has got just one testicle, and he is talking about having a glass one inserted, just like a pedigree dog.

I don't mind his vanity. But won't it be cold to the touch?　　　　*R.B. Ilford.*

FIONA: *It won't be hanging there like a clacker. It will be surrounded by nice warm, skin.*

─────────────

■ I ASKED my boyfriend what it was like to be gobsmacked, and he hit me. I don't regard that as very nice. Should I still see him?

　　　　L.N. Manchester.

FIONA: *Any man who raises his hand to a woman should be thrown back in the sea.*

─────────────

■ ME and my boyfriend got ourselves dog-knotted the other night and had to call for help to separate us. It was very embarrassing. Does this happen often?　　　　*T.N. Redcar.*

FIONA: *No, but it's enough to waise the woof when it does!*

─────────────

■ I WORK unsocial hours, basically nights, and don't get up until the afternoon. I find it extremely difficult to chat up women at this time of day, as their minds always seem to be on other things. Like shopping and suchlike. What can I do?　　　　*A.S. Manchester*

FIONA: *Most girls like it best at that time of day!*

Rooms service

"GHOSTBUSTERS" at Nottingham University have been called in to investigate the case of the Maid and the Missing Rooms.

For the servant spectre appears to have spirited away 14 rooms from 14th century Carnfield Hall in Derbyshire.

New owner, Jim Cartland has been assured the derelict house has 49 rooms – but he can only find 35.

Now the students hope to follow the ghostly maid as she creeps up the stairs nightly, in the hope she will lead them to the missing ones.

AMAZED scientists believe they have discovered an entire city built by space aliens . . . on the surface of MARS.

New research into shock photos taken by an American space probe has revealed strange rock formations on the planet are really part of a space colony the size of central London.

And the ET town is situated just a few miles from the famous Mars Face — a huge monument believed to have been carved by bored space aliens half a million years ago.

The mile-long 'face' made world headlines when the mind-blowing photographs were first released — but boffins have now revealed the city was ALSO made by little green men.

"The objects appear to be carved by intelligent design and not by the random forces of nature," revealed Dr Mark Carlotto of Boston's Analytic Science Corporation.

"It is extremely unlikely that it is a trick of light or shadow," he said.

Dr Carlotto came to his stunning conclusion after using computers to plot a three-dimensional image of Mars's surface from photographs taken by NASA's Viking probe.

Experts say the settlement has its own city square, scores of derelict buildings, an alien fortress and even a huge five-sided PYRAMID.

And incredibly, an E.T. standing in the city's centre would have been able to watch the Martian sun rise from EXACTLY behind the stone face.

"Geologically, the odds are one in 500,000 that this would be here by chance," revealed Richard Hoagland, founder of scientists' organisation The Mars Project.

But eggheads say Mars CANNOT support native life — and the city, situated in the planet's Cydonia region, was probably built by visitors from another galaxy.

"There is a school of thought which says a group of extra-terrestrials known as the Space Brotherhood selected many thousands of years ago," revealed British expert Geoffrey Keats, of the Crystal Research Foundation.

"They were very advanced beings from a very distant part of the Universe. If that was the case then these findings would almost certainly be linked with the Brotherhood.

"The city was probably built by the extra-terrestrials as some sort of stop-off point before reaching Earth."

Amazingly, the huge pyramid located to the south-east of the main settlement may have been a giant TELEPHONE, which aliens used to speak with their pals back home.

"A lot of people believe our own pyramids in Egypt were built not so much for burial purposes but were really huge radio receivers for communicating with distant stars," revealed Geoffrey.

"The Martian pyramid may have been constructed for similar purposes and the aliens may also have built pyramids.

"But it would have taken technology far more advanced than our own to achieve such a thing," he added.

Now scores of top scientists and astronauts are hoping to send ANOTHER space probe to Mars to gather more information about the city.

"There is so much uncertainty about the origin of these objects that they should be a major target for future spacecraft that are sent to Mars," said former astronaut Dr Brian O'Leary.

"We must get back and photograph them at a higher resolution."

The amazing city first showed up in pictures taken over 10 years ago — but have been almost ignored until now because sceptics refused to believe it was anything more than weird rock formation.

As seen through our telescope

THIS amazing picture — seen through Sunday Sport's special super high-power telescope — clearly shows an ancient alien city.

On the left, position "A" marks the main living area of the Martian metropolis, while "B" is the City Square where ETs met to swap snippets of intergalactic gossip.

Left of centre, position "C" reveals a fortress built to fend off the air attacks which some experts say account for the planet's crater-scarred surface.

The mile-long face is in the centre, marked by "D", with "E" showing a cliff face, and "F" pinpointing the five-sided pyramid.

Bomber lost in space

FEARS were growing last night for the safety of the World War II bomber pilots lost in space.

The top-secret Shuttle mission to rescue them last weekend backfired when the TOW ROPE broke.

After Atlantis touched down empty-handed in California on Wednesday, White House officials were quizzing the five astronauts over their mission's failure.

"The President is furious," said an insider.

"They'd nearly got it back into the atmosphere when the damned rope snapped and the bomber went floating into space."

Officials at Cape Canaveral are STILL maintaining the top-secret mission was to set up a spy satellite.

But we shattered the world by revealing the REAL mission was to track down the missing bomber — last photographed in a crater on the Moon in August.

● To be continued

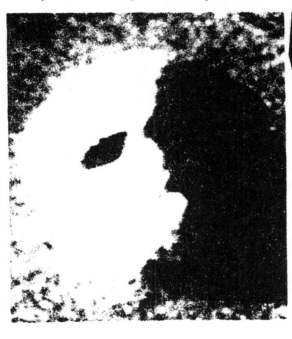

Facing facts

EXPERTS believe this amazing human face was carved by members of an ancient Martian civilisation.

The sculpture measures an incredible ONE MILE long, and may have been chiselled out of solid rock more than 500,000 years ago.

Satellite pictures taken by NASA's Viking space probe caused an international storm when they were first seen back on Earth.

Scientists now say the chance of the carving being a freak of nature are 300,000 to one.

And they believe its position so close to the Martian city prove it was made by alien hands.

A snooze in the loo

HOUSEWIFE Rose Hillier enjoyed a tot of vodka before she went shopping, and ended up in court after falling asleep in Sainsbury's loo.

Police were called after people wondered why the cubicle door was locked for so long.

The 36-year-old Thatcham woman was later fined £10 by magistrates at Newbury for being drunk in a public place.

Devilish

THE coven in your Sex for Satan story last week sounded more like an orgy!

You called it evil, but I think it sounded a great laugh.

That moaning Kevin Carlyon is a right pagan in the neck.

Phil Rogers, Cardiff.

FRANKENSTEIN DOC'S SEVERED HEAD HORROR!

A FRANKENSTEIN doctor wants to chop off human HEADS and hook them up to a weird life-support machine that can be plugged into the mains in your living room.

If potty Professor Robert White gets his way:
● Grandma could happily carry on chatting to the geraniums in the greenhouse long after her body is DEAD;
● And grandpa could whizz around the house in a specially designed wheelchair controlled by his BRAIN.

The madcap American medic has just come to Britain in a bizarre bid to convince our own brain surgeons that "If you want to get ahead... get a HEAD!"

Weirdo White, 62, has even talked to the Pope about the religious ethics of his amazing operation.

For more than 25 years the dotty Doc has been hacking up laboratory monkeys and swapping their heads and bodies around.

Paralysed

The crazy quack, who is head of neurosurgery at Ohio's Metropolitan General Hospital, has confessed that even though the new bodies could keep the heads alive, his freaky experiments have left the monkeys paralysed from the neck down.

"Unfortunately I have been unable get the brain to link up with the spinal chord, which would give the monkey the ability to move around," admitted Prof White.

We stick out our necks to get the top exclusives

By BILL CORKE

Now American lawyer Chet Flemming has patented a machine which he claims is capable of supporting a HUMAN head.

"It could provide the perfect solution for Professor White," he claimed.

"The heads would be able to think, remember, see, hear and talk. The concept of the brain living on after the body has died is truly staggering.

"I know at least half a dozen people prepared to live as machines. They are all either paralysed or their bodies are dying from diseases like cancer.

"With this machine you could conceivably have a head controlling voice-activated computers which are already capable of operating wheelchairs and robotic arms."

But last night the professor was branded a monster by the world's biggest campaign group against animal experiments.

Stephen McIvor, of the British Union for the Abolition of Vivisection, said: "White is clearly off his head. His sick nightmare vision belongs to the Chamber of Horrors.

"He should be locked up. God knows what will happen if he gets his hands on humans."

FIT OF PEAK

SAUCY Sunbather Maria Americio, 29, was beaten to death with a rock — for exposing her boobs to an outraged onlooker at a mountain resort in Andorra.

No sweat

WELSH arts chiefs didn't see the joke when one of their shops started selling bottles of 'Dylan Thomas Sweat'.

The bottles, which proclaim "Your prayers have been answered — the Bard lives — Dylan Sweat" have now been taken off the shelves of the Arts Council's shop in Cardiff.

TATTOO THEIR WILLIES

A TORY MP is demanding that AIDS victims should have their willies tattooed as a warning signal.

And Geoffrey Dickens wants carriers who still sleep around to be castrated.

The 55 year-old backbencher spoke out after reports that some twisted AIDS victims deliberately spread the disease to get their revenge on society.

Mr Dickens, MP for Littleborough and Saddleworth stormed: "When you are fighting a killer you need drastic action.

"These people are committing manslaughter, or even murder. Some of them

By Chris Roderick

are only carriers and can live forever while their sex partners die.

"They should be castrated if they don't tell their partners. All options to stop them should be considered — and that includes branding their private parts with a tattoo."

A lawyer for Atlanta's AIDS Task Force in the States has already suggested branding irresponsible carriers as a warning to potential lovers.

Said James Ceile: "They should be offered a choice — to be kept in quarantine or be branded — where only a sex partner would see the warning."

But the British Medical Association branded the idea as "horrendous".

A spokeswoman said: "The way to prevent the spread of AIDS is to make people more responsible."

He's stuffing me for loving!

MY LOVER has a thing about fatter women — and he's fattening me up to meet his specifications.

I have fried bread, three sausages, two eggs and potatoes for breakfast, a Chinese dinner at lunchtime and a vast fry-up in the evening.

Then we go down to the pub and he insists I drink pints of stout.

Whopping

I've gone from a trim eight stone to a whopping 13 stone in three months, and he is still not satisfied.

None of my clothes fit,

I've busted all my bras, and I get wind so often it's an embarrassment.

I'll do anything to keep my man happy.

But I'm worried that if I lose my lover, I'll never find another.

My legs have purple blotches, my skin is deteriorating and I have three wobbly chins.

It's true, I have tits like the front bumper of a car, but that may not be enough to meet a new chap.

What should I do?
P.W. Peterborough.

FIONA: *Consider your health, love. All that fat you eat could lead to heart problems, and you must feel ill.*

Tell your man you're not going to stuff any more for him.

And if he won't accept that, go on a secret diet, and when you reach target weight, get a new chap in your sights.

Just hissed off

A SNAKE slipped from a vacuum cleaner and hissed at houseproud Bob Deighton when he went to tidy up.

The harmless American garter snake was caught by police after sleeping at driver Bob's home in Fleet Street, Derby.

"I though it was a plastic toy until it stuck its tongue out," Bob said.

GIANT JELLYFISH ATE MY FAMILY

MANEATER . . . jellyfish

A GIANT jellyfish leapt from the sea and gobbled up a woman and her two children ... claims the man accused of their murder.

Maintenance worker Henri Baiselle, 38, says the juddering monster from the deep swallowed his wife and kids whole in a terrifying attack.

Police have arrested Baiselle but he's sticking to his fishy story about the quivering beast the size of a car.

He claims the jellyfish attacked wife Ellane, 34, and youngsters Phillipe, 12 and Catherine, 10, as they took a dip in the sea on a family holiday in France.

But his incredible claims have baffled investigating detectives because they put him on a lie detector that showed he was telling the truth.

By JAN HARDY

"My daughter was swimming in the sea when she started screeming. Her brother went out to see what was wrong and Ellane followed," Baiselle said.

Powerless

"Then they all started screaming and I swam out too. When I got near them I saw the horrible monster.

"It was a huge jellyfish the size of a car, and it was sucking them all inside it.

"They were surrounded by cloudy, white, jelly-like material. They were trying desperately to pull themselves out but the monster kept sucking them in.

"I grabbed my wife's hand but I was powerless against the strength of the creature. It finally sank back into the water taking my family with it."

The bodies of the three have never been found and there have been reports of larger than usual jellyfish in the area.

Donor father weds daughter

A BUSINESSMAN who donated sperm in 1966 has just discovered his new 20-year-old wife is his daughter.

"I wouldn't have dreamt this could happen, said Sherman Helms, 42.

Now after blood tests confirm his new wife is his daughter the Canadian wants a divorce.

Lovers' shock dousing

TWO young lovers in bed got a shock when electrician Gary Hockley burst in — and doused them with a bucket of water.

Pretty red-haired Anita Burton cowered topless as Hockley and her boyfriend. Andrew Robertson, grappled with each other.

And when she tried to intervene she was punched in the face, magistrates at Guildford, Surrey, were told.

Hockley said he put a damper on the lovers because they had been talking about him and his girlfriend behind their backs.

But it led to him being fined £125 and ordered to pay £125 compensation after he was found guilty of assaulting Miss Burton and causing criminal damage. He was bound over to keep the peace.

UFO shocker...
ALIEN BABY KEPT IN A JAM JAR!

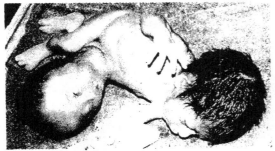

SON OF SATAN . . . Mehmet before the op.

EXCLUSIVE By BILL CORKE

SURGEONS who chopped off an ALIEN baby's extra head have put it in a JAM JAR.

And last night it was revealed the grotesque, amputated head is to go on show to medical students in the Turkish capital of Ankara.

Experts are hoping to pinpoint what caused it to burst out of tragic tot Mehmet Aydin's chest — just like in UFO sci-fi film Alien.

Mehmet, who survived the miracle surgery, is back home with his parents where he's made a remarkable recovery.

Doctors were devastated when his severed head carried on LIVING for almost three hours after the life-saving operation.

But now scientists are planning to carry out bizarre experiments to make sure such a birth never occurs again.

Peasants in a remote mountain village formed a lynch mob to destroy the pathetic little boy when they learned he'd been born with two heads.

Even the youngster's own parents were convinced they were cursed by the Devil, and their monster child was a "Son of Satan".

As the tiny tot was being prepared as a freak human sacrifice, he was grabbed by his quick-thinking granny, who whisked him to the safety of a hospital 200 miles away.

After the unique operation, surgeon Gazi Aydin got permission to keep the extra head.

Since then, it has been stored in a jar in the pathology department of Diyarbakir Medical Hosptial, in eastern Turkey.

Laboratory technicians have preserved the head in a mixture of salt water and formaldehyde — an embalming fluid which can also be used to kill slugs.

The eyes, which had under-

developed retinas, have already been removed and are being studied by opthalmic boffins.

"There are many tests still to be carried out on the head and I am arranging for it to be shipped to Ankara," said Dr Aydin.

"In the interests of medical science, further examination of the head may prevent a birth like this from ever happening again," he added.

A member of his surgical team said: "We are completely baffled by the whole astonishing business..

"Everyone was astounded when the separated head survived for hours after it was amputated.

"The entire world of medicine is eagerly awaiting the outcome of further experiments."

■ A baby born with a 3,000-year-old silver chain around her ankle has been hailed as living proof of reincarnation.

Aisha Sabry's birth at a hospital in Alexandria, Egypt, is now being investigated by stunned scientists.

JOHN WAYNE GHOST SAVED MY LIFE

QUIET MAN . . . Wayne floats around yacht

BIG John Wayne's ghost rode back from beyond the grave . . . to save the lives of shipmates aboard his luxury yacht!

For as the Duke blazes across the telly screens in True Grit tonight, the star's spirit is believed to be secretly sailing the high seas off California.

By GAZZA THOMPSON

And the new owner of the late hero's boat Wild Goose confessed last night: "John Wayne's ghost saved my life!"

Amazed lawyer Lynn Hutchins says a stetson-wearing phantom, believed to be Big John, guided the 500-ton converted minesweeper to safety in high winds.

Watching

"John's looking after his property and watching over me," revealed Lynn, a top attorney in Los Angeles.

"You can't spend too long on the yacht without feeling his presence annd knowing he's around."

Incredibly, Lynn says dozens of crew and passengers also owe their lives to the Western star.

For the huge yacht broke free as passengers whooped it up at a wedding party on board but the boat drifted AGAINST winds to safety in Newport Bay, where Big John's private dock used to be.

"There were thousands of small boats in the harbour and the yacht would have just smashed them to pieces," he said.

Love is – 57 wives

POLICE arrested a 50-year-old Romeo as he married . . . for the 57th time.

And the man later admitted he also had a staggering 228 mistresses – and "I love them all".

Now the randy Iranian has been told by Ayatollahs that even though having more than one wife is legal, he's gone over the top.

HAVE you been an alien's plaything? Do you:
● Suffer from the same nightmare every time your head hits the pillow?
● Panic about going back to a place you visited but don't know why?
● See the same handsome stranger in your dreams?
● Think you've had a crazy experience but can't figure out where and why?

If you answer yes to all these, Jenny reckons you've had an away day with an alien.

LUCAN SPOTTED ON MISSING SHERGAR

Highland fling for elusive earl

FUGITIVE Lord Lucan is alive — and galloping through Scottish glens on missing Shergar.

That's just one of the amazing claims from hundreds of readers who say they've spotted the wanted murder suspect.

After we revealed the runaway toff had phoned Sunday Sport, our office was flooded with letters from readers claiming they'd sighted him — everywhere from Lands End to John O'Groats.

EXCLUSIVE By JEREMY PHILLIPS

"I've just returned from a holiday in the West Highlands of Scotland and I saw Lord Lucan several times on my morning walks," claimed Ian Wray, of Southampton.

"He is in the vicinity of the Kyle of Lochalsh area and can be seen early in the morning taking his daily ride on Shergar," added Ian.

Takeaway shop worker Mark Campbell claimed he'd spotted the infamous Earl on holiday in North Devon.

"While I was in my shop on Woolacombe Beach, he called in and bought a cup of tea.

Surprise

"About five minutes after he'd left I realised who he was," said Mark, of Ilfracombe.

Reader Tony Lombardelli's eyes stood out like organ stops when he saw our picture of Lord Lucan.

For he recognised him as a chum who he sends copies of Sunday Sport to in Canada. That could explain why the Earl chose to ring us — he's an avid reader of Britain's brightest Sunday paper.

"Lucan's new name is Lee McFarlane and he lives in Toronto, Canada. Study the photograph of him and you will see Lucan and McFarlane are one and the same," said Tony.

"The moustache is still there and — although he has since dyed his hair and put on a bit of weight — the beady staring eyes give him away.

"He is now living with an older woman who refuses to talk about her lover's true identity."

● We're still giving a £10,000 bounty to anyone who can PROVE they've found Lord Lucan.

So if you think you've played darts with him at the local boozer for example, drop us a line at Sunday Sport, 50 Eagle Wharf Road, London N1 7ED. Please mark all correspondence "Lord Lucan."

Keep your eyes peeled — he could be your milkman, boss, neighbour . . . or even your best mate.

● IS this Canadian Sunday Sport reader really the runaway Lord Lucan?

George's jibe at TV gays

GENDER-BENDER pop star Boy George has lashed out at EastEnders' gays Colin and Barry for being a pair of misery guts.

"I get annoyed when I watch EastEnders. Colin and Barry are always arguing," George said.

The reformed junkie says a true gay would rarely ditch his long-time lover and days later go out with a girl.

Earlier miserable Colin was seen frolicking with busty barmaid Pat.

George added: "One goes off with a woman but it doesn't happen all the time. Going off with a man is different and always a problem."

Millions of viewers watched Barry storm out of Colin's flat and walk straight into the arms of Donna.

PET HATE

SICKO movie Pet Cemetry in which dead dogs rise from the grave is set to shock animal lovers in Britain after breaking box office records in America.

No foolin'

A MAN who saw a giant UFO hover over his village has convinced police he is not trying to fool them.

Mid-Glamorgan officers were told the object was as big as three houses and had rows of flashing lights.

2-FACED WOMAN SMOKES 140 A DAY

WORLD EXCLUSIVE

By CHRISTINE RODERICK

TWO-FACED wonder Francine Mailland last night revealed she's so nervous about people giving her double takes, she gets through 140 fags A DAY.

By an incredible quirk of nature Fran, 28, was born with TWO full faces.

And that means she can inhale on one side — and blow smoke rings out the other!

Taunted

In her teens, Fran was so sick of being taunted she kept BOTH profiles low.

But now she's hit back: "Don't call me a monster — it's not my fault! I was born like this.

"I've got one body and one heart. But who's to say two faces aren't better than one," said her

● **TURN TO PAGE SEVEN**

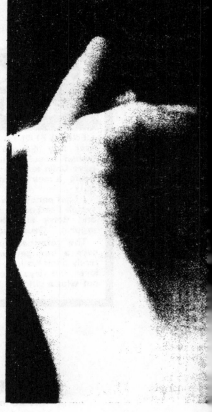

No man has gone

LOONY Leftie women's libbers have zapped the final male frontier of cult space show Star Trek.

Despite series bosses' desperate bids to keep the world-famous Trekkie phrase: "To boldly go where no man has gone before," campaigners have forced them to drop "no man" for "no-one."

A show spokesman said: "It's totally illogical."

Breedin' cock up

BONKING beings from outer space have got their love lines in a tangle.

Shocked UFO-spotters have been told how amourous aliens anxious to breed with us are going for the WRONG targets.

In one recently reported abduction, sexy spacemen on the look-out for nookie beamed up a lesbian by mistake, according to author and UFO reseracher John Rimmer

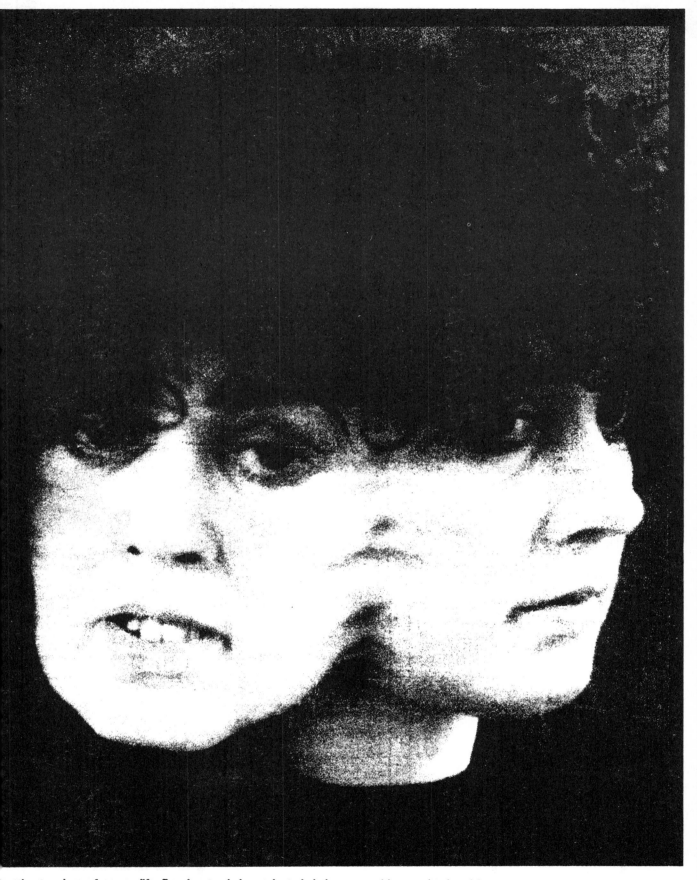

putting two brave faces on life, Fran has to chain smoke to help her cope with a cruel twist of fate

THE INCREDIBLE DWINDLING DOG

TWINKLE TOES the tiny Pekinese is a pint-sized pooch with a difference . . . she's shrinking by the day.

The amazing diminishing dog is so small she easily fits into a champagne glass.

And little Twinkle Toes has to spend most of her time trying to avoid the local cats — unless she wants to be mistaken for an appetising mouse.

Her astonished owner Betty Inwood reckons that any day now the eight-week-old pup will be able to nestle inside an eggcup.

Twinkle Toes is an incredible 2½ inches tall and weighs in at a featherweight 12oz.

Her fast-growing brothers Snowboots and Snowstorm are already a sturdy 3 lb — the normal weight of a miniature Pekinese.

Baffled Betty, who has bred Pekineses for 30 years, said: ''At first I thought my eyes were deceiving me. But as her coat gets bigger she seems to shrink.

''Soon her coat will be too big for her. She can easily sit in a Babycham glass, but if you try her

■ **A measly 2½ ins high, weighing 12 oz — and still shrinking**

■ **Twinkle Toes dare not leave home — or she could become cat food**

By BRIAN ANDERSON

in anything else she disappears.

Her feet and legs are as small as my fingernail.''

Betty, of Chesterfield, Derbyshire has tried giving the cute canine giant meals. The pup jumps into the bowl, vanishes amongst the food and happily munches the lot.

But despite her huge appetite, Twinkle Toes just keeps on getting smaller — and nobody knows why. Not even a vet has been able to help.

Accident

Betty added: ''Because she is so small, I have to carry her around with me all the time.

''If I left her alone with her brothers they would probably squash her by accident.

''She sleeps in a tiny cabinet because her legs are not long enough to climb into a dog basket.

''I can't let her out in case a cat gets hold of her and has her for supper.''

Meanwhile, Twinkle Toes continues shrinking. Betty said: ''I just hope she doesn't disappear altogether — she's worth £250.''

■ RASH punters are grabbing a slice of the action in a new betting craze – pig racing!

One Hampshire farmer has even set up his own trotters track in a field.

One fan said: "It's a great sport. When the animals are no good to race any more, you can always eat them."

Love feast
SAUCY Birkenhead shopkeeper Gerry White has snapped up £2,000 worth of aphrodisiac ''royal jelly,'' said to have spiced things up for Prince Andrew and Fergie.

COUPLE STUFF

WE LIFT THE LID ON CASE OF REAL TERROR

SEX SLAVE IN BOX FOR 7 YEARS

Evil pervert keeps maid under bed for sick lust

STONEWALLED!

NEWLY-WEDS Rose and Vic Mychajlow found pals had bricked up the doors of their new home in Shelton Lock, Derby.

They left a gift-wrapped hammer for builder Vic to break in.

Presley was a caveman

SCIENTISTS have discovered the remains of a tribe of prehistoric apemen whose features are identical to rock king Elvis Presley.

The resemblance is so stunning that boffins think the legend could be a direct descendant of the Stone Age swingers.

The amazing evidence was unearthed when egg heads reconstructed the face of a skull found in Africa.

"It's the damnest thing I've ever seen!" said archeologist Dr Otto Rohde.

But last night Elvis fanatics were up in arms at the suggestion that their idol is descended from a caveman choir.

"It's a dreadful thought to imagine these prehistoric men walking around in glittery suits shaking their groins at naked cavewomen," said fan Nick Kelly.

HELPLESS housemaid Colleen Stan told last night how a twisted sex monster stuffed her in a coffin under his bed . . . for SEVEN years.

Evil carpenter Cameron Hooker turned pretty Colleen into his sex slave and kept her chained and gagged in the house where his wife and kid lived.

And as terrified Colleen lay fighting for breath in her tiny prison, sicko Hooker made love to wife Janice just inches above.

Pretty Colleen eventually became so brainwashed by evil Hooker that she even signed a contract AGREEING to his sordid whims.

"He hung me up and whipped me. I thought I was going to die," she said.

Now, as pervert Hooker rots behind bars, his victim has told for the first time of how she was:

● KIDNAPPED by evil Hooker as an innocent hitch-hiker, aged just 20.

CABLE EASE

GOBSMACKED builder Alvin Glaze fell 180 feet without breaking a single bone in his body. He plunged from a Los Angeles skyscraper, but managed to slide down support wires.

WUFF 5 YEARS FOR DOGHOUSE WIFE

Crufts dog show shocker

Cruel kennel creep hubby is collared

DISTRAUGHT mum Maria Jesus led a dog's life for FIVE YEARS . . . after her evil carpenter husband chained her up in a HOME-MADE kennel!

And even daughter Celia had a WUFF time in the doghouse as crazed woodcutter Jose Jesus kept his family without food or water — because he couldn't trust them.

DOG'S LIFE . . . Maria

"It seems he didn't have much faith in either of them. He's just like that by nature," said a stunned police spokesman.

Each morning, the evil monster caged the pair before he left for work, locking the doors, windows and even the fridge behind him.

The 64-year-old beast lashed Celia and Maria to chairs and beds and threatened to beat them up if they tried to flee the house in Salvador, Brazil.

Now Celia, 23, suffers from a mental illness after the ordeal and can only scramble

By SIMON FINLAY

around on ALL-FOURS.

"She was a perfectly normal girl before all this. We suspected something was going on in the house, but we never really knew what," revealed a shocked neighbour.

"Both of them were in a terrible state when they got out. It seems they were kept in awful conditions."

The neighbour added: "My wife noticed that Maria never went out shopping to the market with other wives . . . but she never dreamed things were that bad.

Police burst into the horror kennel and released the 59-year-old mother and her daughter, after an anonymous caller tipped off a local radio station.

Now carpenter Jesus has been locked up for five years himself, after a Brazilian court found him guilty of caging his family.

But incredibly the jealous fiend denied he had done anything wrong!

"They must be crazy, those chains and ropes were being used for some work I was doing at home," he told police.

PET LUCK!

BURGLARS got such a warm welcome from luckless householder John Sartor's two guard dogs that they emptied his Brooksville, Florida, home — and stole the mutts, too!

Ghostbusting Doc's hooked on spooks

GHOST-BUSTER GP Simon Dein is running an amazing moonlight express around Britain's haunted graveyards.

And he's keeping his patients in the dark about his spooky after-hours sideline.

The dotty South London doc is coining in the cash with coachloads of ghost-hunting tourists queueing up for seats

BATTY . . . Dein

on his monster-mash minibus.

"If my patients found out they'd think I was a bit barmy. But really it's all good clean fun," said fearless physician Simon, 28.

His Psychic Tours company has become a graveyard smash offering £17.50-a-time romps around cemeteries and black museums – guaranteed to send a shiver down the spine.

Strokes of pure genius

IF you want to be a better bonker, get in the swim.

A top sex scientist has proved it's the perfect cure if your love-life has gone down the plug-hole.

Phillip Whitten discovered the secret of sex-cess after carrying out a survey of 160 competitive swimmers.

He found swimming gave people a new lease of life in the love-stakes — even at the grand old age of 80!

Water-babes between the ages of 40 and 80 were having sex as often as people half their age.

A staggering 100 per cent of the swimmers he interviewed in that age group made love at least once a week.

The average figure for non-swimmers is a measley 60 per cent.

And the tide turns in favour of swimmerers when it comes to enjoying themselves between the sheets, too.

Whitten found 88 per cent of the women and 98 per cent of the men over 60 had a better time in bed compared with averages of 65 to 86 per cent for the landlovers.

Whitten believes the reason may be because swimmers keep in trim and know they look good.

He said: "These people were proud of their bodies and they felt younger".

55-INCH WHOPPA BLOWS KAMA SUTRA LEGEND

2,000 years of history explodes

BIG-BUSTED Susie Sawyer revealed last night how her 55-inch whoppas forced her to discover an all-new Kama Sutra.

For centuries, nookie experts have claimed there are only 64 ways to have sex, and listed each one in the Kama Sutra – the Bible of bonking.

But Susie's gigantic curves made traditional rumpy-pumpy impossible – and drove her to invent 37 NEW positions not in the book.

"My husband couldn't get near me because my boobs were so big," confided the buxom Midlands housewife.

"But now I've come up with 101 mind-blowing ideas on how to cope with colossal curves between the sheets.

"The first thing I had to do was to find a way of stopping my massive knockers getting between me and my man.

"I tried tying them up with string, but it kept snapping," confessed Susie who found her whoppas weighed 7lbs EACH after plonking them on the bathroom scales.

"Finally I got the idea of slinging them over my shoulders, and that did the trick – but not before one little disaster . . .

"The first time I tried it, my left one came bouncing back and hit me smack in the face. I was knocked out cold," admitted the sex siren.

YOBS FROM SPACE STOLE OUR BOOZER

FUN-LOVING aliens were last night nursing out-of-this-world hangovers after beaming up an entire village pub for an incredible inter-galactic booze-up.

The invaders from outer space struck shortly before closing time yesterday as they swooped over the London and South Western Hotel, Exeter, in a huge, cigar-shaped craft.

Shocked eye-witnesses told how a pulsating red beam enveloped the whole pub as it drifted up into the sky.

Beauty consultant Christine Meakin was preparing a cheeseburger supper for her boyfriend as she glanced out of her kitchen window and saw the fantastic sight.

"All of a sudden the air turned terribly hot and, without warning, the pub floated up into the clouds. I could hardly believe my eyes," she said.

"There was a very loud humming sound and I was shaking in terror."

The whole astonishing incident lasted only five seconds before the pub arrived back down on Earth in the sleepy Devon village of Topsham, said Christine, 36, who lives 300 yards away.

Gardening aliens get down to Earth. . .

GREEN-FINGERED aliens landed at a posh stately home — and stayed to mow the lawn!

And then the inter-galactic gardeners rolled up the sleeves of their space suits and did a spot of weeding too.

They just couldn't resist tending the wide open spaces at luxurious Newstead Abbey, near Nottingham.

Two couples witnessed the bizarre scene — and both claimed they saw dome-headed extra-terrestials glow while they worked.

The terrified tourists stood rigid with fear as the aliens pottered around the rosebeds, humming a haunting tune as they snipped off dead flowerheads.

Nottingham's UFO expert, Dennis Harriman, is investigating the amazing close encounter.

"I have a report that two beings not from this planet were rooting around the gardens at Newstead Abbey," he said.

"I understand they may even have taken some examples back to their own planet."

Drunk

But space-lagged locals who were sucked up in the amazing pub-nap say they spent at least two hours drinking and gambling with the boozy beings.

Computer consultant Gerry Richards, said: "There were about 40 of these little red men and they got boozed out of their minds.

"One minute I was talking to my mate at the bar, the next I was knocking back pints of Guinness with this crazy bunch of three-foot-tall aliens.

SPACED OUT. . . Richards

"They spoke perfect English, although their voices sounded a bit tinny. They were not too unlike humans, although they had no hair and their legs were sort of rubbery.

"All the time they were laughing as they told the landlord to pour them more beer. They must have drunk at least 300 pints. It was unbelieveable."

Landlord Ray Mabbutt, 36, lost his temper at one point when the extra terrestrials tried paying for their booze with luminous sugar-cube currency they called Gdonks.

Pub chef Derek Hitchcock, 42, said: "It's the first time I've ever served bangers and mash to a bunch of aliens, but they lapped up the lot."

Last night village bobby Mike Dommit said: "I've been in the police force 19 years, but I've never dealt with a case like this. Everyone I've interviewed has told the same story. It must be true."

DUSTMAN QUITS AFTER ALIEN IN BIN HORROR

A DISGUSTED dustman last night revealed how a gang of ALIEN lager louts hounded him out of his job.

And binman Stephen Roberts said he'd rather face the dole than the foul-mouthed space yobs who made his rubbish round a living hell.

The 40-year-old refuse collector was sick of being rubbished by drunken green spacemen.

Father-of-two Stephen claims the hungry ET-lookalikes are prepared to travel thousands of light years to feast on the rich pickings in Britain's dustbins.

The brow beaten binman reavealed how scores of space aliens are living in dustbins all over his home town of Nottingham.

"I quit! These aliens are a bloody menace," stormed Stephen.

"They are all over the place living secretly in dustbins."

Stunned Stephen's horror began when he lifted the lid on a bin to find an angry alien inside — gorging itself on table scraps.

"It was a hell of a shock to see this green, three-foot alien covered in rubbish," he said.

Swore

"It had a saucepan on its head and was eating a Cornish pasty.

"In my panic I picked up a rotten apple and slung it at the horrible creature.

"It swore at me, leaped out of the bin and levitated over a house. I was amazed."

But instead of beaming itself back home the hairy little alien called on his pals for help.

Overnight, dozens of inter-galactic thugs started turning up in dustbins all over the town.

"They must be hungry,

SCARED... Stephen

because they eat all sorts of rubbish," said Stephen.

"Us dustmen get the blame if there's litter strewn all over the place, but it's the untidy aliens who do it.

"A lot of them are drunk and I've seen them chuck their empty cans into the streets.

But despite the space yobs' hooligan antics, Stephen claims they are cowards at heart.

"They're wary of burly binmen," he revealed.

"They might pick on old ladies, but one look at an angry dustman and they're off."

Yet the little green things DID eventually scare Stephen off. Now he plans to buy a boat and sail across the Atlantic in a bid to escape the fiends.

A spokesman for Nottingham City Council said: "Our refuse collectors don't often look inside the dustbins.

"The rubbish is usually just thrown into the back of a refuse vehicle, so we aren't aware of reports of aliens as such."

It's cheapy Charlie!

BARGAIN-hunting Prince Charles has been snapping up dozens of freebie glass tumblers at his favourite petrol station.

The thrifty motoring royal has even entered a garage raffle in a bid to win a turkey.

The future king picks up tokens which entitle him to cheapo whisky tumblers for every £10 worth of petrol he buys.

Owner John Branston, whose Bradfield Garages in Tetbury near the Prince's Highgrove home have won the royal warrant, said:

"I'm amazed the Prince bothers to collect the tokens.

"But I don't think they come in just for free gifts. We are competitive and four star's just 165p a gallon."

Mad wife kept dead hubby as a mummy

NUTTY nurse Carol Stevens kept her mummified hubby's body in a bizarre house of horrors for NINE years . . . waiting for him to come back to life!

The weirdo wife changed shrivelled Carl's pyjamas every day before propping him up in bed for his daily wash.

*Picture: Paul Davies
The Garden Studio*

RANCID . . . how humming hubby Carl looked to cops

And she rubbed creams and ointments into his stinking flesh to keep it fresh.

"Carl looked like a piece of freeze-dried fruit," said stunned cop Mark Shearer.

Carol got her young children to join in the strange ritual of tending to Carl's body . . . by exercising his joints before going to school.

They even built a secret tomb for their office clerk dad after he mysteriously disappeared from work.

Cops sent in to probe 36-year-old Carl's vanishing act in 1979 were told by Carol he'd become ill — and she was looking after him.

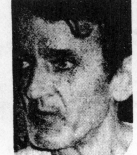

CULT . . . Richard Kunce

Decomposing

They sincerely believed he'd come alive again," said Knox County's Sheriff Shearer, who investigated the case in Galesburg, Illinois, USA.

"They had some sort of drainage system so the decomposing flesh inside could be flushed away."

Diabetic Carl died when he halted his insulin injections after being introduced to an odd holistic health cult by dentist Richard Kunce.

"Kunce moved in with Carol in 1986," said Shearer.

"They decided to remortgage the house, so Carol forged

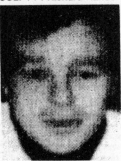

MUMMIFIED . . . Stevens

Carl's signature and Kunce was witness to it."

At an Illinois court Carol, 45, was given two years probation for forgery, failing to notify a coroner of Carl's death and cruelty to children.

Kunce, 57, was given 30 months probation.

CHEAT DAY

A PASSENGER who pretended to faint, to avoid paying his fare, legged it from Basingstoke station before an ambulance arrived — to the amazement of staff and travellers.

Saucy nun reveals her dirty habit

A GOD-FEARING nun has walked out on the sacred celibacy of a convent . . . and written a sex manual.

Pretty Jenny Newman of Liverpool shunned strict vows and pious worship and is now living in unmarried sin with her boyfriend.

Last night the Catholic church slammed the frank book, but the former nun claims steamy seduction is women's strongest weapon in the battle of the sexes.

Jenny, 41, shunned her clean convent life and married her tutor at Liverpool University during the swinging 60's.

Jenny eventually divorced the tutor and now she's written the saucy book.

I'VE FARTED SO I'LL FINISH!

COCKNEY Mastermind hero Fred Housego told last night how petrified contestants BREAK WIND uncontrollably in the dreaded black chair.

The chirpy taxi driver said normally prim and proper brainies lost ALL CONTROL once they sat in the spotlight.

Fred, who found fame and fortune after he won the BBC contest, which celebrates its 300th show tonight, revealed the amazing secret — which even Magnus Magnusson has kept under wraps.

Now he's turned "I've farted, so I'll finish" into a household phrase.

"Unless you let rip with a massive under-the-sheet megablaster, which would blow down the Walls of Jerico, you

Master blasters exposed

THE BITCH ON THE BOX

EDITED By CHRISTINE RODERICK

can get away with it," said jovial Fred, 44.

Fred, the most famous Mastermind champ in its 17-year history, won eight years ago to become the first working class hero to collect the coveted brain-teaser trophy.

He became a top-flight celebrity, rubbing shoulders with the stars and presenting LWT's hit Six O'Clock Show

with Michael Aspel.

Now he runs a lucrative tour guide business, drives cabs, and appears on radio and TV while still reading up to FIVE books a week.

And in an amazing FOUL-MOUTHED outburst, Fred shattered his calm, brainbox image by revealing his HATRED for passengers he picks up in his cab.

"Some of them think that the second they step in they've won the bloody taxi," he ranted.

"The best thing to do with people like that is to stick two thumbs down their throats."

WINDY . . . not Fred Housego

Cosssby!

THE Cosby Show on Channel 4 used to be a sight for sore eyes on Sundays.

Fast-moving, some good jokes and witty scripts.

Now it's a pathetic piece of self-indulgent pap with about as many laughs as a trip to the dentist.

Scrap the show, Bill. Please!

Mumbles

HAS anyone ever watched an entire episode of Miami Vice . . . and understood it?

It's not the plots which are complicated — it's Crockett and Tubbs' amazing, illiterate mumbling.

And, to cap it all, in walks their hilarious Mexican boss, who talks as though he's got an ashtray stuck in his mouth.

Gnome soaks up the sun

NOBBY the garden gnome stunned his owners during the heatwave . . . by turning golden brown.

Gobsmacked owner Ken Jones, 50, of Port Talbot, South Wales, said: "I thought I was imagining things. But he's the talk of the town now."

Gnome manufacturers Willowstone say a sun-sensitive paint is to blame for his tan.

BIRD BRAINED

TOP BOFFINS are persuading rare falcons to have SEX with them by wearing bird-shaped hats! The falcons BONK the bowler and the sperm's collected for artificial insemination.

ALIEN CURRY BEAST BIT MY BUM

ANOTHER RED-HOT EXCLUSIVE

. . . while I was sitting on the loo!

CURRY addict Bob Germanek bit off more than he could chew the night he became a Vindaloo victim of a bum-biting alien!

Last night engineer Bob, 26, flushed with horror as he recalled the extra-terrestial toilet terror that left him constipated for a fortnight.

After guzzling down a steaming hot curry, ten poppadums and six chapatis, he was forced to make a call of nature in the loo at his council house in Stoke-on-Trent, Staffs.

But when he lifted the lid on his lavatory, all hell broke loose as a slimy green space monster slithered up from under the seat.

"I was scared out of my wits," said a blushing Bob.

"I felt a sharp nip on my bum and, when I jumped up, I saw this frightening being staring at me from the toilet bowl.

"It had glaring eyes, three rows of snapping teeth and reared up, dripping green slime all over the bathroom floor."

Quick-thinking Bob acted like lightning in his one-man Star Wars to destroy the dirty green gremlin.

"I grabbed a lavatory brush and clobbered the thing smack on the top of its head," he revealed.

"At first the monster

BITTEN . . . Bob

appeared dazed and slid back down and around the U-bend."

But, seconds later, the raging E.T. reappeared and threatened to slop out over the floor and engulf him.

"I had no choice but to squirt the alien with a bottle of bleach," said Bob, still trembling after his ordeal.

Bomber fever grips Britain

THE whole nation's gone bomber barmy — and that's official!

Phone lines at Sunday Sport have been red hot since we printed the amazing picture of a World War II bomber on the moon last week.

We've been deluged by letters from the mind-boggled millions who've been racking their brains over our out-of-this-world shots.

The question on everybody's lips was IS IT TRUE and, if so HOW DID IT GET THERE?

And our answer, as we pointed out in the article, is we DON'T KNOW!

FLASHBACK . . . April 24

You certainly came up with some great solutions such as:
- store manager Jim Brown from Southampton who said: "There's no doubt it was kidnapped by a UFO. These extra-terrestrials will stop at nothing to find out more about the human race."
- Cook Peter Davis from Cardiff: "I argued out this one with my mates in the pub for hours and we think it's not a picture of the moon at all but a massive lump of cheese."

Of course, some of our more sceptical readers went for theory THREE — that the picture was a brazen fake.

Either way we're over the moon that the shock satellite pictures got our imaginations running wild.

Granny's feet off the deck!

A GRANNY was recovering in hospital last night after being SWALLOWED whole... by her DECK-CHAIR!

Luckless Dirgit Linder became entangled in the carnivorous canvas chair after going on to her balcony to lap up the sun.

She got more than she bargained for — and spent TWO DAYS trapped with her head jammed between her knees.

Police eventually freed her from the potty predicament after a nosey neighbour had spotted her sitting in "an odd position.

"I was just lying there for hours and hours. I could not move a muscle," the 80-year-old told baffled docs in Malmo, Sweden.

"It was the worst 48 hours of my life."

A police spokesman explained: "The chair's cloth was rotted by the weather and tore as she put her weight on it.

"She could not get up and she could not use her hands to free herself."

ANGLER CAUGHT BY MUTANT FISH

You'll be reeling at this exclusive

A BURLY angler told last night of how HE was caught by a mutant fish.

Water bailiff Brian Ellis — who weighs in at a mammoth 16 stone — couldn't believe his eyes when he pulled in the snarling pink monster.

For the evil creature, the size of a large cat, jumped out of his net and RAN OFF using its fins as legs.

At first, brave Brian dashed after it. But the fierce fish reared up...and chased HIM instead.

"It was a really evil-looking thing with blood-red eyes," gasped Brian.

"I'll never forget the moment when it reared up and stared at me.

Flapped

"It looked like a wild animal ready to pounce. Then suddenly it shot towards me and went between my legs. I didn't half move, I can tell you."

As Brian flapped around in terror, fellow anglers helped capture the angry fish by throwing a giant towel over it.

TERROR...Brian

Brian agreed to put it in the giant aquarium at his home in Osbourne Road, Liverpool.

"I locked it in a great big tank with a huge aluminium lid on top to stop it getting out," said Brian.

But as he slept that night, the fish CLIMBED out of the tank and died while trying to escape.

"Somehow it had managed to get the lid off," said Brian.

"It had dried out and died in the middle of the room!

Confirmed

"I found it in exactly the same position as when it had reared up on its fins — looking as if it was ready to pounce."

Now scientists have CONFIRMED Brian's fishy story after experts from the Natural History Museum in London examined the remains.

The strange creature is believed to have been a mutant albino version of a fierce Indian Catfish.

"We believe it was tipped into the canal by a local tropical fish shop owner who went bankrupt," said the museum's fish expert Alwyn Wheeler.

GRANNY FROM OUTER SPACE KEEPS ALIENS IN HER ATTIC!

SILVER-HAIRED pensioner Dolly Newland confessed to an amazing secret last night . . . she's the granny from OUTER SPACE who keeps aliens in her attic!

Granny Newland was zapped down to earth 70 years ago — and has kept in regular contact with her intergalactic brood ever since.

As top Ufologists were racking their brains over Dolly's claim, the ET granny called on Sunday Sport readers to WELCOME little green men with open arms.

"They're all very friendly — all they want to do is have a chat," revealed Dolly, 76, sitting beside the fire at her cosy North London home.

Invisible

"I love them. My dog Sandy knows all about them and doesn't get annoyed when they come to visit me.

"But nothing annoys me more than scientists poo-pooing everything and saying that UFOs don't exist. I KNOW they do."

Space granny Dolly says most of her fellow aliens — some of which are INVISIBLE — would never harm humans and are SHY at heart.

"As soon as somebody gets excited, they're off," revealed Dolly, who has known her amazing secret since she was only eight.

ZAPPED . . . Dolly

"I was with my grandfather in 1921, when I saw what I thought was a shooting star going past the moon," she revealed.

"My grandfather told me not to point at it — or the men from space would visit me."

But naughty girl Dolly disobeyed her grandad and WAVED at what turned out to be a passing space-freighter.

Little green men have been visiting her ever since — and, sometimes, they keep her awake at night by stomping around her ATTIC.

Incredibly, Dolly says we ALL have a little bit of alien in us.

"You'd be surprised how many of us are descended from them — through reincarnation. I know I am.

"That's why they're so friendly — they've been to this planet before in the distant past," said Dolly.

"They're very worried that we're going to destroy ourselves, with all these bombs and everything."

BASIL FAWLTY NICKED MY BRAIN

Fan turns into clone of Cleese

CRAZY... Stewart welcomes the Germans

A GANGLY guest house boss who named his establishment FAWLTY TOWERS kicked his waiter last night and sobbed: "Basil Fawlty stole my BRAIN!"

The crazy clone confessed: "I can't help it — the character is taking me over."

Stewart Hughes is so OBSESSED with his manic hero — immortalised by John Cleese — he now even fears for his MARRIAGE.

"God knows how long my wife Sybil — sorry, I mean Joanne — can put up with it," he moaned.

Friends say a terrible change came over Stewart since he watched the first episode of the classic telly comedy some ten years ago.

His colleague Bob Ackford said last night: "He was always such a quiet, shy man. But he began to be transformed after watching the shows."

Bob, 62, added: "He rants

By JOHN GARVEY

and raves at the guests and he is incredibly rude.

"*We opened a restaurant on the premises last week, and he made me head waiter. But he BEATS me all the time, and keeps calling me Manuel.*

"We had a party of German

visitors here last night, and Stewart immediately began chuckling to himself and sidling over to their table — and I remembered what happened to the Germans in the show.

"Basil ended up doing Hitler impressions. We only just stopped Stewart in time."

Incredibly, the restaurant at the Fawlty Towers guest house in Sidmouth, Devon, is THRIVING — despite Stewart

---

Bette's legged it to fame!

BUSTY stunna Bette Midler has confessed she got her big break ... by showing off her LEGS!

For Bette — whose new movie Beaches is storming British box offices — says wearing micro-skirts helped launch her career.

Whoppas

"I also said things people were afraid to say — and that's how I became famous," said Bette, 43, now one of the world's best comedy actresses.

Bette, who flashed her whoppas on stage at the London Paladium, even married her German hubby ... because he was BALD!

Double-up

COMPANY director Brian Davies bought a hallway in a Bath house two months ago for £15,000. He's now selling it for £30,000.

Zapped by alien arcade love

FOR months I lusted after the beautiful buxom blonde in the local amusement arcade.

I would watch for hours from behind the one-armed bandits, marvelling at how nimbly her fingers manipulated the joystick.

The arcade was deserted that wet Wednesday afternoon when our eyes met.

She asked me if I fancied a two player game and I readily accepted.

She went first and I leant over her admiring her rounded breasts as her erect nipples pushed against her flimsy white T shirt.

As she shot hordes of aliens she became progressively more excited, sighing and gasping as she saw off wave after wave of attackers.

I think that perhaps she sensed my bulging manhood as I leant against her pert buttocks.

After what seemed an eternity she finally got zapped and it was my turn.

Imagine my surprise when I felt my own joystick being pulled from side to side as I struggled to fend off the invaders.

Soon we were writhing on the arcade floor, as I fired wildly in all directions.

The trouble is, we've now both been banned from the arcade, and so now I have to play at home with my own joystick.

How can I see her again?

P.J. Liverpool

FIONA: *Why not invite her round to your house? Then at least you can play without being interrupted.*

Beware of the bullshit

BULLSHIT rules in British industry . . . OK yah!

For the nation's Yuppies are swotting up on how to spot bullshit — which is the scourge of business, according to a survey.

The report says senior executives admit managers bullshit staff . . . who in turn bullshit customers.

And the worse bull shitters of all are the Yuppie-infested computer companies, solicitors and accountants.

Bosses use bullshit to hide their failures, conceal facts, create an impression of power and keep staff from leaving.

Yuppies are warned to beware of their sweet-talking bosses.

Mummies horror

A PSYCHOPATHIC salesman who strangled his parents and hid their bodies wrapped like mummies in cooking foil has been sent to Broadmoor indefinitely.

The couple, brewery worker Mr. Evyln Lynch and his wife Elspeth had been missing for a fortnight befor being found by police in a garden shed last April.

Their son, Barbados-born Dennis Lynch, 32, admitted manslaughter by reason of diminished responsibility at Reading Crown Court.

Lynch, of Prospect Street, Reading, told detectives how he strangled his 50-year-old mother with a length of rope and used a knotted cord to kill his father, aged 55.

There had been a family dispute beforehand.

SARDINES FROM OUTER SPACE

HORRIFIED Harold Degen told last night how his home was invaded — by FISH from OUTER SPACE!

Hundreds of the scaly aliens beamed down to Earth in the middle of his back garden.

The silvery sardine-sized spaceman rained down from an eerie black cloud which suddenly appeared over mechanic Harold's quiet country home.

> **' Even our cat thought there was something fishy about the visitors ,**

"I just couldn't believe it," he said. "I started quivering and shaking, I was so scared.

"I began to run for cover but it was too late. All around me were hundreds of tiny silver fish."

The invaders are believed to have been heading for a river 40 miles away from his home in Victoria, Australia.

But their navigation went wrong — and their planetfall ended in disaster when all 800 of them exploded on impact.

We always catch the BIG tales!

Harold and his wife Debra puzzled over what to do with the bodies.

"We decided to feed them to our cat Samantha," he said.

Boffins

"But even the cat thought there was something fishy about the visitors."

Weather boffins confirmed that similar mysterious showers of fish have happened all over the world.

Alien expert Rex Dutter, editor of the UFO magazine Viewpoint Aquarius, says they come from Venus.

"They've been appearing on Earth for millions of years," he said. "But they're friendly. If they wanted to conquer us they would have done it long ago."

Last night Britain's top alien expert Rex Dutter blamed the planet Venus for the invasion.

"Their mind power means they can take any form."

■ BAFFLED boffins don't know why extraterrestrial fish continue to visit our planet. Here are three possible reasons:
1. Inter-galactic fish tanks collide with passing meteors and send their passengers hurtling to Earth.
2. Pea-brained inhabitants of the far-off planet Pisces are desperate to mate with humans in order to boost their intelligence.
3. These fish may not be aliens at all. Some scientists believe freak winds whip up fish from rivers, depositing them miles away.

Experts rocked as they conclude...

BORN-AGAIN Elvis Presley found true love — behind a stack of tin cans in a supermarket.

The not-so-dead King of Rock 'n' Roll made the startling admission during a taped interview THREE YEARS after doctors pronounced him DEAD.

And voice-print experts who tested the authenticity of the kiss-and-tell tape were all shook up last night when they declared: "This is no fake . . . Elvis is alive".

declared: "This is no fake . . . Elvis is alive".

Elvis calmy recounted his sweeter-than-fiction love story during the hour-long interview while he was in hiding on the Pacific island of Hawaii.

ELVIS TAPES PROVE HE'S ALIVE

Interview

"I met a young woman in a supermarket and she kept following me. Finally she said: 'I almost can't believe it, but I think I know who you are.'" Elvis told his interviewer.

"I said: 'Honey if you don't tell anybody I won't'.

"Right then and there in the supermarket she started crying and I said: 'Honey, don't you cry', and the tears just started falling down face."

With his voice trembling with emotion, the King tenderly described how the woman declared her love for him and stopped his heart.

"She put her arms around me and she said: 'I feel I know what you've been through,' and she said: 'I'll always love you'.

"Lord, things like that are experiences you just can't buy and its very hard to forget

EXPERTS ARE CONVINCED INCREDIBLE PHOTOGRAPHS CONCLUSIVELY PROVE . . .

ELVIS IS ALIVE

EXCLUSIVE — more amazing pictures inside

LAST WEEK . . . our exclusive story.

anything like that," added Elvis.

During the interview Elvis also told how he is planning to make a comeback and is brushing up his act in readiness for the day the King returns to reclaim his crown.

"Lately, I've been trying to write music, which is something I've always wanted to do — I guess I never took

the time before," he said.

"I still play the piano and I'm trying to play the guitar better. I spend most of my time getting myself into shape."

Album

Despite pleas from his loyal legion of fans, Elvis feels the time is still not right for him to put on his blue suede shoes and tell the world he's back.

But he plans to call up some of his closest music-biz pals when he's ready to record the album which says he is now writing.

"I mean to get all the people who've helped me in the past to help me with the new album. It would have to be the biggest experience of my life and I'm certain it will be good for them too," he said.

● IS ELVIS REALLY ALIVE! Judge for yourself by listening — for the FIRST TIME — to our amazing taped interview.

Why be lonesome tonight when you can listen to the world's greatest LIVING LEGEND.

NECKS, PLEASE

HEARTBROKEN barber Sal Phillips accidentally BUTCH-ERED his best friend yesterday... because he SNEEZED while shaving him. His mate fell asleep, and Sal slit his throat in Rome.

EXPERTS ARE CONVINCED INCREDIBLE PHOTOGRAPHS CONCLUSIVELY PROVE . . .

ELVIS IS ALIVE

EXCLUSIVE — more amazing pictures inside

LIVING PROOF . . . a picture of the King and his doctor taken just weeks ago

By CHRISTINE RODERICK

AN Elvis Presley sensation last night rocked the world when experts saw this amazing picture and declared: ''The King IS alive.''

For the exclusive shot was snapped — along with others — just a few weeks ago.

They show Elvis's personal doctor, Elias Ghanem, with a mystery in Las Vegas. Photo-experts confirm the prints have NOT been tampered with.

And 11 years after the King's alleged death, Ghanem has set Memphis alight by admitting: ''Yes, I was there.''

World-famous Elvis researcher Maria Columbus said: ''What more proof do we need that the King is alive?''

Elvis's daughter Lisa Marie has yet to see the evidence which could jeopardise her multi-million pound fortune.

LIVING legend Elvis Presley has spoken for the first time about why he faked his death.

That is the astonishing conclusion from voice print experts who tested an amazing message from the King recorded YEARS after he was supposed to have died.

The moving confession — published exclusively in full today — tells in chilling detail how Elvis:

- Is working flat out on a comeback LP.
- Hopes to go public over his hoax funeral.
- Has been haunting supermarkets, football matches and large crowds wearing a long grey beard.

The TAPED phone call follows hot on the heels of amazing photos, hailed last week as conclusive proof the King is still alive.

And now experts are saying the King has SPOKEN. At the Voice Identification and Acoustic Analysis Centre in Texas, specialists say the voice print ties up with known tapes of interviews with Elvis.

And it's been proved the world-shattering conversation was NOT placed together from old Elvis chats.

"The date of the conversation is never mentioned," said Elvis investigator Gail Brewer Giorgio, who was handed the tape in confidence.

"But by the contents of the tape I believe it was done after August 16, 1977, because of what he says.

"The two women who gave me the tape really didn't want to say too much, for personal reasons."

In the secret recording, Elvis speaks of his heartbreak away from daughter Lisa Marie, now married and pregnant.

The voice claims he STILL sings and STILL takes lovers.

And THIS is what he says about the faked-death "getaway" from fame:

"It actually started when I arrived in Hawaii. I made arrangements with a friend of mine to come out of the state.

"It was really something, because everything worked just like it was meant to be."

He goes on: "There was an island that I had learned about a long time ago and I

guess I always knew that some day I would probably have to use it.

"I needed the rest even more than I knew.

"It's very hard to stop doing something that you've been doing that long — after a year I started missing the people and entertainment.

"It's been a question of growing beards — and this and that — to keep from being recognised.

"As far as enjoying life, I've been at ball games and the movies, but what interests me most is seeing people in a way that I hadn't before.

"It would be foolish to walk back into a lifestyle that

I'd just escaped from."

In a lazy Southern drawl, Elvis hesitantly talks of his hankering to reveal himself to his daughter Lisa Marie and his old Memphis buddies.

Amazingly, he says a host of associates already know about the hoax but have kept his secret life under wraps.

And in another piece of chat said to allude to Dallas star Priscilla Presley, he says it's too soon to go public.

"As far as she or any member of my family is concerned I really don't think it is a good idea right now," he says.

"It makes me happy just to see that she's all right.

"You know, a lot of times people have come up to me and said they are concerned about my people and family finding out. But they usually say that nobody will believe them anyway."

Elvis shocks fan with his new disc

ELVIS-MAD Alan Osman last night said his idol is alive and has released a smash-hit record.

The single, called "HONEY" was proved to be GENUINE after exhaustive tests.

Alan, 33, said: "When I heard it I knew it was Elvis.

"I got the shock of my life when RCA records tested it and confirmed it was ELVIS and had been recorded after his alleged DEATH."

Alan, of Tottenham, London, asked Sunday Sport to tell the world of his discovery, because he's sure we are Elvis' favourite paper.

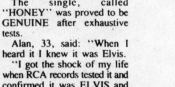

How the King ended my drug hell

TEARFUL housewife Lillian Evans told last night how she wept at our Elvis pictures saying: "Yes, I've seen him.

"It was three years ago — and HE SAVED MY LIFE."

Lillian, 52, kept her amazing story close to her heart, but now the Plymouth mother-of-three has admitted: "I

was in hospital at the time feeling incredibly depressed.

"I was trying to stop taking tranquillisers. Suddenly, in the middle of the ward, Elvis walked up to me wearing a white suit and shoes.

"He convinced me to stop taking the pills. He told me to go back to better ways."

Let's see his body!

SHOOK-UP Elvis fans have jammed our phone lines demanding to know if the King IS alive.

A campaign's mounting to dig up the King's grave after last week's living-proof pictures.

"If the family's so sure he's dead, why don't they prove it to us?" stormed Elvis fan Elaine Liddel, of Sheffield.

"There's been so many sightings it's time to dig up the King's body."

But Chris Barfour, from Burnley, is a believer. "Who was the mystery Elvis look-alike watching the funeral?

"I think Dr Elias Gharem should be tailed."

Steve Zodiac, from Shrewsbury, was intrigued: "I just hope he IS still alive. Can you get him over to Britain?"

EXHUME. . . says Elaine

ELVIS TELLS OF HIS FAKED DEATH

PILOT FUELS UFO SIGHTING

GOBSMACKED villagers thought the Martians were coming when a giant fireball lit up the night sky.

Police were swamped with calls from people who said they had seen a UFO near Upper Heyford, Oxon.

The US Air force said a pilot jettisoned fuel when his undercarriage stuck - and the after-burners ignited it.

LIVING DEAD STUNS DOCTOR

PRONOUNCED dead, an electrocution victim began breathing again 40 minutes after a doctor had given up a 45-minute attempt to revive him. The doctor, in Wichita, Kansas, said of the 47 year old man: "He was very, very dead. He was deader than a doornail."

ELVIS PRESLEY ALIVE... posing as a woman

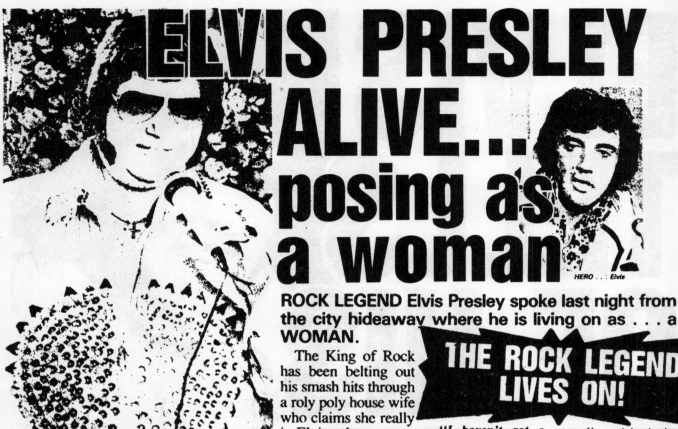

LOOKALIKE . . . Jutte in her Elvis stage gear

HERO . . . Elvis

ROCK LEGEND Elvis Presley spoke last night from the city hideaway where he is living on as . . . a WOMAN.

THE ROCK LEGEND LIVES ON!

The King of Rock has been belting out his smash hits through a roly poly house wife who claims she really is Elvis reborn.

And even though every song comes out in GERMAN, 48-year-old Jutte Jeuthe scoffs at suspicious minds, saying: "I'm absolutely convinced . . . I AM Elvis.

The 14-stone Elvis lookalike wants to be crowned QUEEN of rock after fans declared: "She ain't nothing but a Hound Dog — and she's Elvis down a tee."

Powers

But Jutte, who downs a Memphis diet of peanut butter, ice cream and burgers for that King-size look, can't explain why the songs don't come in English.

"I sing in German and Elvis sings through me," she said through a translator.

"I first realised my powers 30 years ago and I've been in love with him ever since.

"I haven't got a boyfriend. I have given my heart to Elvis. I spend all my time thinking about him. There's no time to think about other men."

Her home in Hamburg is like a monument to the swivel-hipped rocker.

There are Elvis paintings, clothes, pillows, records, guitars and photos in every nook and cranny.

Dresses

Jutte even has an exact replica Elvis's, guitar with King Elvis emblazoned across the fretboard.

She dresses like him, wears her hair the same, and surrounds herself with Elvis memorabilia.

"It's as though Elvis's ghost is alive inside me and and has taken me over." explained the dumpy singer, a dead ringer for Elvis in his later years.

"He has even spoken to me at times from the Spirit World, and every day of my life is devoted to him."

Flesh

She's been to his Gracelands, Memphis home EIGHT times and will never forget the day they met in the flesh in his dressing room after a concert.

"He told me he loved me, and I'll always cherish that memory." she sighed.

ELVIS BALD, BROKE AND ALIVE IN BRITAIN

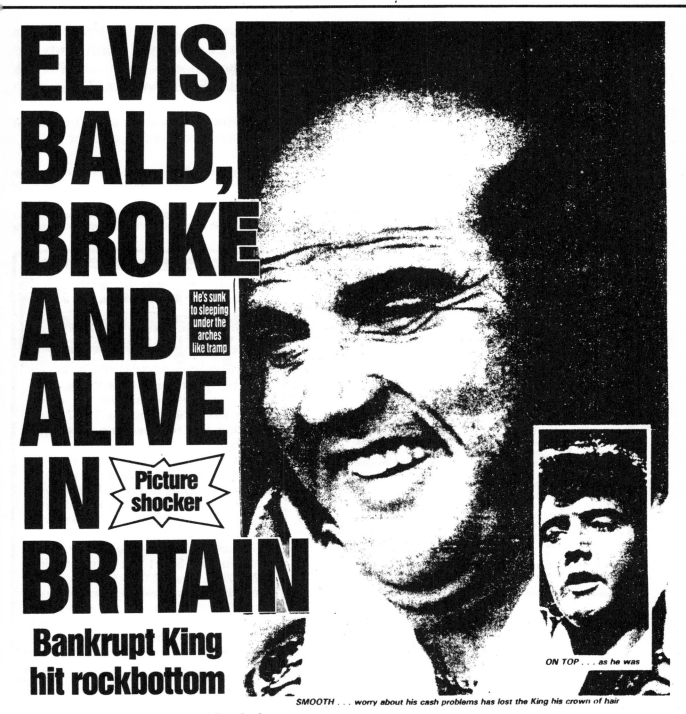

He's sunk to sleeping under the arches like tramp

Picture shocker

Bankrupt King hit rockbottom

SMOOTH . . . worry about his cash problems has lost the King his crown of hair

ON TOP . . . as he was

ELVIS Presley, the King of Rock, has been found **BALD** and living like a **TRAMP** in London's dosser land, it was revealed last night.

An incredible THIRTY-EIGHT plastic surgery ops have left Elvis a haggard down-and-out, exclusive photographic PROOF has shown.

Bankrupted by the cost of surgery, the King's once shiny black hair has fallen out with worry, leaving him bald as a COOT.

These astonishing claims have been confirmed by this world exclusive photo of the King. Sunday Sport experts believe it COULDN'T for forged. It was taken this week under London's infamous Charing Cross arches, where tramps shiver the night away in cardboard boxes.

Presley pops up to see star Rick

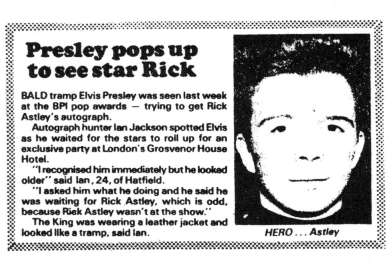

BALD tramp Elvis Presley was seen last week at the BPI pop awards — trying to get Rick Astley's autograph.

Autograph hunter Ian Jackson spotted Elvis as he waited for the stars to roll up for an exclusive party at London's Grosvenor House Hotel.

"I recognised him immediately but he looked older" said Ian, 24, of Hatfield.

"I asked him what he doing and he said he was waiting for Rick Astley, which is odd, because Rick Astley wasn't at the show."

The King was wearing a leather jacket and looked like a tramp, said Ian.

HERO . . . Astley

Dowdy housewife Elizabeth Prince last night blew the Elvis legend apart with the astonishing revelation — "I lived with the King four years AFTER he FAKED his own death."

And stunned scientists backed her sensational claim when Liz was wired to the latest foolproof lie detector test . . . and PASSED!

Now for the first time she is ready to tell her rock 'n' roll shocker which proves Elvis Presley conned the world with his gruesome death so he could lead a normal life.

As millions of faithful Elvis fans plan to make the pilgrimage to his Graceland home in Memphis on Tuesday to mark the 11th anniversary of his death, Liz's startling story will send them reeling.

Yesterday the softly spoken 41-year-old told how a hunky singer with greased hair, quiff and sideburns she met in a seedy bar in 1978 was the pop idol the world had "buried" a year earlier.

She revealed how Elvis hoodwinked his adoring fans into believing he had died by:

● sneaking out of Graceland while a life-like waxwork dummy was smuggled in to play the role of the dead King

● conning medics into thinking a dead wino was really him

● leaving everything to his daughter Lisa.

"I was in a naval club when I met the man I later knew to be Elvis," whispered Liz.

"I got to know him and soon we became lovers," she confessed.

"After a few months we began living together. He was kind and polite and an excellent musician."

For an amazing four years the couple toured little known clubs in towns, where the guitar man with the sensational voice drove crowds wild.

From 1978-81 hundreds of club goers were watching the King of rock and roll belting out the old Elvis numbers from Hound Dog and Blue Suede Shoes to Love Me Tender — but they never knew who he was.

"He could mesmerise his audience. People would travel 200 miles to see him. He always had a following," said the one-time barmaid from Atlanta, Georgia.

Shared her bed

But it was several months before she realised the man who shared her bed was Elvis — her teenage heart-throb.

"One night he seemed nervous and secretive and I thought he was running around with another woman," admitted Liz from the cosy living room which was the King's secret hideaway.

"He started crying and said he couldn't live a lie anymore. He told me he was the real Elvis Presley and said how his death was planned a year in advance."

And as she looked deep into his earnest blue eyes, Liz knew he was telling her the truth.

"He was the same height and weight as Elvis. He had the same hands and auburn colour hair," she revealed.

"He wore a beard to disguise his looks but he had all the physical characteristics of Elvis," she said.

And in a shock revelation she admitted that the King was still a junkie.

"He still had a drug problem," she said in her hushed Southern drawl.

"Wherever we travelled three men always went with us. They took care of things and they'd bring him prescription drugs if he wanted them."

They kept a discreet distance but Liz recognised their faces from Elvis's early days when they had been his faithful minders known as the Memphis Mafia.

For years Liz kept the King's sensational secret and the couple lived as man and wife with Elvis using her surname.

"He was all the things you have ever heard Elvis was," she confessed with a sigh.

I LIVED WITH ELVIS FOUR YEARS AFTER HE DIED

Rocker was my boyfriend, says Liz

Dancing to a disaster

A TRENDY club that has invited young lovers to bonk the night away on Valentine's Day has been blasted by the town's top doc.

Dartford medic William Charlesworth has warned Flicks disco the crude call to throw caution to the wind could cause an AIDS epidemic.

But a club spokesman said last night: "We don't know what the fuss is about."

Steamy sex cure

A BONK a day can keep the doctor away, according to top sexperts.

Their randy tips — which allegedly help cure pains in private parts — could leave delighted couples bonking barmy in their search for health and vigour.

The raunchy revelations come from Sexual Secrets, a steamy new book by Nik Douglas and Penny Slinger.

A bridge too far

A SNEEZE cost Ray Castle his brand-new false teeth.

They shot from his mouth, skidded along the gutter and dropped down a drain in Gotmanhay, Derbyshire.

Works supervisor Ray, 47, called in council workmen who retrieved the dentures, but their special pump had chewed them up.

Glum Ray said: "I wish I'd used a net."

EVIL satanist Alex Sanders, kinky King of the Witches, almost took an astonishing sex secret to his grave. . .

He was the first ever to have sex with A MERMAID!

The amazing revelation which has sent shockwaves across the world was made last night by the warlock's close companion Derek Taylor.

Warped wizard Alex himself once confessed he had enjoyed a sordid seven-month fling with the incredible half woman, half fish.

Alex admitted during his dark, black magic days he lured the mysterious sea creature from her safe sea-bed into his massive water water bed where he kept her as his salty sex slave.

He trapped the innocent ocean virgin for months so he could go down in history as the first human to have a mermaid as a live-in lover.

Even though Alex used the phenomenal fish as his sex object to live out his twisted fantasies, his massive sexual appetite soon tired of the aqua-lass, and he chucked her back into the sea.

But before he grew bored with the Piscean sex-pot, he often raved of the special pleasures of mermaid love. . .

*"Have you ever f***** a fish?" he asked members of his coven.*

"If you haven't, I suggest you buy a big one and try it."

Those were the only tell-tail signs he ever gave the world about his amazing scaly lover.

"I lived with her for seven months and she was very beautiful," he confessed before he died.

And his close friend, Derek, revealed Alex used devilish forces to ensnare the mythical creature into his evil web of lust.

"He used his evil power to summon her up. She was supposed to be a witch's familiar — someone that helped him in his work. But she

SPECIAL REPORT
By RUKI SAYID

became a little too familiar," said Derek from his East Sussex home.

The stunning sex siren came ashore in Alex's home town of Hastings, Sussex.

Tantalising top half

In a sensational scene straight out of Hollywood's fairytale film, Splash, the moment the marine marvel left the sea, her powerful 4ft tail magically turned into legs.

Her flowing mane of soft golden hair, huge sea-green eyes and pert, perfectly formed breasts captivated depraved demon-worshipper Alex.

Her tantalising top half and fascinating bottom part made her the catch of the century.

TAYLOR

'He used his evil power to summon her up'

"She was the traditional image of a mermaid," revealed Derek.

"She was beautiful and graceful with liquid eyes that melted Alex. She was his ultimate fantasy."

And as the amazing creature fell under Alex's powerful spell, she turned tail on her secluded sea world and ditched her fish friends to become a landlubber.

Scores of Alex's witch chums never guessed the cool blonde with the clammy handshake was a real-life mermaid.

The tell-tale signs that she was a sea-creature were there — but covens never twigged.

Liberate goldfish

Undime — a witch word for sea-creature — came close to giving away her deep secret when:
● She dived into plates of mussels and guzzled them without shelling them first;
● Tried to liberate goldfish by tipping them out of their bowls and down drains;
● Sat glued to the TV when oceanic documentaries come on.

KING OF WITCHES

SLEPT WITH A MERMAID

'If you've never had it with a fish I suggest you buy a big one and try it'

ALEX SANDERS

Steak-out

A SPOOKY spectre has called time on a brewery's hopes of turning his haunt into a Beefeater steak restaurant.

Whitbread's plans for the old paper mill in Croxley Green, Herts, have been abandoned because the spirit frightens site inspectors.

I MET JESUS IN HEAVEN

PENSIONER Percy Collett was in paradise last night, after a cosmic coach trip . . . to HEAVEN.

Perky Percy, 86, told how an ANGEL whisked him up to meet his maker.

And when he got to Kingdom Come, the out-of-this-world OAP had a bus trip — with JESUS as the tour guide!

"Heaven's a REAL place. It's a planet, like Earth, but it's 80 times bigger, about two million miles round."

The magical mystery tour of the here-after seemed like an ETERNITY, said Percy.

He met his late mum and had a gossip with GOD.

Percy's fantastic voyage took off after he stopped eating and prayed solidly for ten days. And when he went upstairs:

By BRANDON MALINSKY

● HE went to the seaside and walked on the water with Jesus.
● HAD dinner with Queen Victoria.
● BUMPED into Richard the Lionheart and Kaiser Wilhelm.

Missionary Percy's trip happened when he was in the Brazilian jungle.

Although there was a seething mass of SOULS outside, Percy reckons he had no trouble getting in because he was invited by Jesus.

Jesus told him: "Percy, I asked my Father to let you come up here."

"They're building mansions out of gold and precious jewels. They need a lot of them because it's getting rather crowded now," said Percy.

LATE NEWS FLASH: Jesus told Percy he is planning to return to Earth.

STAR-TREKKER . . . Percy

Taylor's garbage for five bucks!

WACKY Yanks desperate to get their hands on superstar souvenirs are snapping up bags full of RUBBISH.

Gift shops in Hollywood are selling off the contents of movie set rubbish bins to gullible tourists.

Labels on plastic-wrapped packages being flogged off say "100 per cent genuine Beverly Hills trash."

Punters picking up the garbage hope they might find items such as Liz Taylor's discarded newspaper, Paul Newman's parking ticket or Tom Selleck's cocktail napkin.

Each bag, costing five dollars, is accompanied by a note reading: "Yesterday the lush life might have been out of your reach... now it's in the palm of your hand."

Sex spell for fertility

CHILDLESS women are becoming pregnant after making love in an amazing pagan fertility ritual.

White witch Kevin Carlyon is organising sex sessions for barren couples on the giant genitals of a pagan hillside painting.

After the bizarre ceremony on the famous Long Man of Wilmington in Sussex, the childless women miraculously become pregnant, claims the 29-year-old witch.

"People approach us who want to have children and we use the figure's natural forces to make them pregnant," he said.

The weird spiritual figure, known as the Long Man, is daubed on a hillside in Wilmington, a tiny village outside Eastbourne.

So far dozens of women have got pregnant after Kevin's weird magic sessions.

HUSBAND CHEATS ON WIFE WITH TORTOISE

He's gone potty over pet

A LOVE STORY THAT'S SURE TO LEAVE YOU SHELL-SHOCKED

ANIMAL-LOVER Mark James left his wife shell-shocked last night when he jumped into their bed with his new love . . . a tortoise called Tootsie.

Mad Mark. 23. plans to hibernate with the creature for SIX MONTHS while wife Julie sleeps in the spare room.

And he's even bought the reptile her own electric blanket so she won't get cold in the long winter nights ahead.

"There's no way she'll be alone in a box of straw this winter," said the wacky warehouseman.

"When she opens her little eyes I'll be there by her side, and she'll have to comfort of a double divan, feather pillows and an electric blanket.

"Nothing's too good for my Tootsie, whatever anyone else has to say."

Mark has made up hundreds of lettuce and tomato sandwiches to feed his dozey date while outside temperatures plunge below zero.

But outraged Julie reckons the affair will never last.

"For the life of me I don't know what he sees in her. Goodness knows what the neighbours will think," she fumed.

"I don't fancy spending the winter in the spare bedroom playing second fiddle to an ashtray on legs."

Mark's winter nights of pet passion also startled reptile boffins at London Zoo. They don't think Tootsie will wake up before mid-May . . . but if

SALAD DAYS . . . Mark's going well with shell

she does. Mark's the one who'll feel a nip.

"If a tortoise is awoken or slightly disturbed during hibernation they will do everything possible to defend themselves." said expert Norman Rich.

"They're not used to being in a bed, and this man could find himself with a nasty bite. I wish him the best of luck — he'll need it."

But Mark — who fell for Tootsie during long walks around his garden in Stillitoe Place. Stoke-on-Trent — is determined to carry out his weird winter watch.

"I know she loves me by the way she nods her head and winks." he confided.

"At first she was shy, then she started coming out of her shell. Now we are inseparable.

SEXY NAT'S FATHER IS KING WITCH

EXCLUSIVE by MARK SOLOMONS

STUNNA Natalie Banus hides an incredible horror movie secret... the man she called dad is a witch who has cast black magic curses on his enemies.

And her nightmarish upbringing by the warlock who dubs himself Emperor, King of the Witches, involved playing weird games of tarot with her when she was an innocent 14.

At ten, sorcerer Alex Sanders allowed his schoolgirl step-daughter — who shot to fame through Sunday Sport — to witness the magic christening of her real life mum Gill as Queen of the Witches.

"I have cast ack magic spells for revenge,"

admitted 72 year-old self-confessed bisexual Sanders, who sends messages "backed with magic influence" to his star step-daughter.

"I've hurt people through my magic," said five-times married pagan king Sanders from his home in Bexhill, Sussex. "But not killed them."

The sinister Emperor is a follower of the bizarre Wicca group — a sect that follows pagan rites reaching back before Christ.

"I don't see Christ as the messiah of the world," he added and said of the naked midnight rituals he has had: "It's the way the ceremony is meant to be performed."

Emperor Sanders, who claims to be the most powerful witch in all Europe, divorced Natalie's mother earlier this year.

But during the four years the family shared a house in the wilds of Sussex, Sanders led magic ceremonies in the kitchen.

Natalie watched amazed as weird cloaked figures paraded in the half-light muttering pagan prayers.

"We didn't want to cross him or get on the wrong side of him, but made it clear he should stay out of Natalie's life," said the 16 year-old model's manager Alan Whitehead.

Meanwhile, as Natalie is abroad on holiday out of her stepfather's reach, Sanders yesterday celebrated the night of the pagan year — Hallowe'en

Dressed in a flowing blue robe, he gathered his followers at a lonely clearing in Ashdown Forest, Sussex, to call up the dead.

"When the moon is full we try to reach out and find those who have gone before us," he said.

SATANIC... Sanders with ex-wife Maxine

CAGED IN COAL BUNKER FOR 20 YEARS

By GAZZA THOMPSON

SHATTERED Tony James last night told of his nightmare ordeal — locked in a filthy, stinking coal bunker FOR 20 YEARS.

The broken 29-year-old spoke days after being rescued from the hell-hole he knew as home.

Haggard and shaking, tragic Tony said his horrific "prison sentence" began when his evil dad chained him up like a dog in a cellar, little more than 8ft wide.

Trembling Tony was fed so little during his misery marathon he was forced to EAT COAL.

"People won't believe what I've been through," said Tony.

"I've been chained up like an ANIMAL and locked away from the world for 20 years.

Stealing

"I thought I was going to die. But I kept going by hoping that one day I'd be free again."

Tony's horror began in May 1969 when dad Jake caught him stealing coal from his family home in the West Country.

Sentenced to a life of black hole hell, his makeshift dungeon consisted of an 8ft by 10ft coal cellar with grime-caked walls and a stone floor.

The only "luxury" he had during his 20 years' solitary was a once-a-week hose-down with cold water.

GRANNIE AND HER AMAZING 10ft NAILS

By PAUL SCOTT

HAVING a manicure can be an all-day job for Lee Redmond . . . her finger-nails are each a foot long.

Grandmother, Lee, 46, began growing her terrific tallons from scratch in 1979.

Now they measure up to an astonishing total of TEN foot.

And despite a TV show's £5,000 offer to cut them off, Lee has vowed to fight tooth and nail to break the 13ft world record.

"I think it's a good thing people like me step out and do the unusual or the world would be a very boring place," she said.

"I'm going to keep on growing them until they're the longest in the world."

Her family have pleaded with her to get rid of the claws.

But Lee said: "They have become a part of me. Having them has meant I have met so many people I would never have met otherwise, and there is nothing I can't do — except play golf because I can't grip the club."

She's got a growing ambition to file for wackiest world title

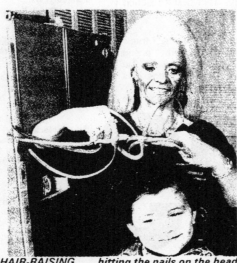
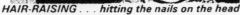

HAIR-RAISING . . . hitting the nails on the head

HANDFUL . . . even washing up is difficult

SPACE ALIENS' BURIAL GROUND

A WHITE-haired widow has been keeping a lonely vigil over the coffin of her alien husband for an incredible four years . . . in The Land That Time Forgot.

And children on the time-warp island use the aliens' graveyard as their favourite playground, explorer Lawrence Blair revealed last night.

Lawrence, 46, and brother Lorne, 43, back from a 10-year adventure to

Children play with the dead

By ALITA MILES

the South Seas, said: "It was an incredible experience for us.

"The whole thing was very spooky, but to them it was totally natural."

The tribe believes the bones belong to aliens who came down from the stars thousands of years ago to start their village.

"They all feel the remains should be well looked after," added Lawrence.

Tiny tots on the remote jungle island take turns to care for the wall-to-wall skeletons in the ghoulish burial ground.

"They lovingly clean and arrange the skulls of their ancestors which, they believe, descended from the skies in spaceships," said Lawrence, from London.

The brothers met the frail 87-year-old Queen of the Toraja tribe on the island who has been living with the body of her husband in a tiny room.

She was forbidden to leave his richly decorated tomb even for a minute in case he felt unwanted.

GHOULISH ... the aliens' graveyard

Ghost buster

A GRUMPY ghost with a grudge against women is wreaking havoc in Pamela Gilbert's antique shop.

The destructive demon has smashed a string of valuable china figures of women in midnight ransacking sessions.

Pamela, 52, now plans to have her 300-year-old shop in Marlow, Bucks, exorcised to get rid of the anti-social spirit.

She said: "We are terrified of what is going to happen next."

The smashing spook has destroyed a £200 china figure, a £300 clock with the figure of a woman on the top, a 1920s "Fair Lady" statue and a painting of a mother and child.

Woman is puffed out

A WOMAN has been banned from smoking in her own home — by a judge.

She had admitted during a divorce case that she only smoked to annoy her husband.

Elizabeth Roofeh was told by the New York judge NOT to light up anywhere near her husband or children ever again, even at home.

SUPERMARKET BOSS CRUSHED MY SPIDER

Creepy killer was so 'cute'

SUPERMARKET bosses were branded killers last night after stealing a deadly black widow spider from a housewife and SQUASHING it.

Nature–loving Valerie Heath was delighted when she spotted the spider in a bunch of grapes she bought at Sainsbury's.

But her joy turned to tears when store chiefs ordered the killer to be destroyed.

Earlier this month housewives all over Britain were put on full alert when an invasion of black widow spiders were found in a

BY BILL CORKE

consignment of Californian grapes.

But last night heartbroken Valerie, of Pestwood Road, Southampton, fumed: "I can't believe what they've done.

"I bought the grapes by weight and as far as I'm concerned the spider belonged to me. They had no right to kill it. It had done no harm. In fact it was quite cute."

Thrilled

Valerie was so concerned for her creepy-crawly Nicknamed Samson that she took it to a local zoo called the Amazon Centre.

"They were absolutely thrilled when they saw my spider because they are so rare in Britain. It would have given them a marvelous opportunity to study such a rare species," she said.

But disaster struck for Samson when officials from Sainsbury's arrived.

Centre owner Pam George said: "This man from the supermarket sounded very official and insisted I hand over the spider. He told me they were taking it to Sainsubury's headquarters in London.

Terrible

"Reluctantly I let him take it, but I had no idea they were going to kill it.

"There was absolutely no point in squashing it. It's such a terrible waste."

Valerie is demanding an apology, but Sainsbury's are unrepentant.

A spokesman said last night: "We needed to retrieve the spider for positive indentification by authorities at the Natural History Museum in London.

DEADLY...but cute. The black widow spider

■ **DINERS in Japan are finding the great British table dressing – horseradish – too hot to handle.**

Doctors have been rushing about reviving scores of Tokyo restaurant-goers who've been collapsing in sweats after trying the newly-introduced dish which is traditional here.

GHERKIN JAR MAN'S BOTTLED UP!

Kinky sex class rap

KINKY sex lessons at a Church of England teaching college have been slammed as bizarre.

Perversion and depravity are on the timetable at the College of Ripon and York St John.

But the chairman of the Campaign for Real Education, Nicholas Seaton, has complained to the college principal and Education Secretary Kenneth Baker.

HUMAN GHERKIN Hugo Zamorathe got so cheesed off with his wife's nagging he climbed inside a PICKLE JAR to shut himself away!

Now the crackpot contortionist has packed his bags and joined a CIRCUS in a desperate bid to escape her constant ear-bashing.

"I've had enough of that woman," Hugo snarled from inside the 14-inch wide jar that's become his home.

"She never stopped complaining from morning to night. So I decided the only way to end all the tongue-lashing was to curl up in one of our pickle jars.

"I'd recommend them to anyone. They're SOUND-PROOF!"

Hugo admits it took a lotta bottle to wriggle his way inside the jar.

SQUEEZE . . . Hugo's home

By BILL CORKE

Now he's earning a living with his amazing body-bending act, travelling with America's Royal Hanneford Circus.

"A couple of years ago, the circus came to town and I took my jar — sorry, my HOME — along with me to show them what I could do.

"They snapped me up on the spot." I could hardly believe my luck", said Hugo.

HOW does he get inside the jar?

Hugo begins with the left leg and then tucks the trunk of his body and his head into the tiny container.

Next, he squeezes his right leg into the jar. The right arm comes last.

Circus owner Tommy Hanneford calls him the "eighth wonder of the world".

"There's no one quite like him." he said.

BOY LIVES IN BUCKET FOR 6 YEARS

Water way for mum to treat her tiddler!

HUMAN syphon Jack Nel has to drink so much to stay alive... his parents have made him live in a BUCKET of WATER.

For Jack, six, is forced to swill down more than TEN PINTS of water a day or he will die of dehydration.

And even when he was just FOUR weeks old Jack had to quaff SEVEN pints a day to keep him going.

"I'm thirsty all the time," says Jack. "I'll drink anything but water is my favourite."

Some of Jack's AMAZING drinking habits include:
● GULPING down his bath water with a straw.
● SWIGGING water straight from the garden hose.
● DOWNING two pints in one go.
● DRAINING his bucket of water time and time again in a day.

Human syphon Jack, from Brakpan in South Africa, suffers from a rare hormone

By GILES LYON

deficiency which top docs can find no cure for except to let him keep drinking.

Drinking

"It was amazing. When he was born he just kept crying for more water," said his mum Magda, 28.

"I got through literally thousands of nappies but he just had to keep drinking.

And when water-baby Jack leaves his bucket in the morning to go to school he has to take at least THREE

TOT... in quart pot

pints of water with him to keep him going until lunch.

The mystery illness, which means Jack's body cannot retain liquid, meant he faced near-certain death when he was born.

KUNG PHEW!

CHAIN-smoking Kung Mingming, four, has been banished from his Chinese home to stay with relatives until he kicks his 40-a-day habit!

Nuke food glows blue

STUNNED scientists have discovered that irradiated food GLOWS BLUE in the dark.

The treatment is meant to kill naturally occurring bacteria in meat and vegetables.

Scientists, struggling to find a method to detect irradiated food, have discovered that, when heated, it gives off a blue glow when the lights are off.

HOUSEWIVE'S KINKY ALIEN LOVE JELLY

He's sick of his parrot

PET shop owner Ray Hanwell is being driven potty by his prize parrot — because it speaks only Spanish.

He bought the bird from a Spanish family who were emigrating — and has never understood a word it says.

Ray, 38, of Hanwell, West London, said: "It could be speaking absolute filth for all I know. I just hope it doesn't put the punters off."

But Ray may have to learn Spanish himself — to be absolutely sure.

BY BRANDON MALINSKY

SHELL-SHOCKED housewife Sheridan Lane has unearthed a sensational space sex shocker . . . an ALIEN LOVE AID.

For the stunned mum claims randy ETs are beaming girls up and smothering them in kinky NOOKIE JELLY before submitting them to frenzied bonking sessions.

The wobbly stimulant is so potent that women just can't resist a big bang with an excited extraterrestrial.

"There are women who discover under hypnosis that they have had intercourse with an alien," said Sheridan.

"They recall being on a spacecraft and having their bodies rubbed with a kind of jelly.

"It's believed that this is some kind of aphrodisiac because no matter how repelled she may be feeling, she somehow feels stimulated at the same time."

UFO-mad Sheridan, 43, reckons the experience leaves human victims with a bun in the oven.

And many of the cosmic kids SURVIVE — but the thieving flying-saucer fiends frequently swipe their half-human off-spring.

SHOCKED . . . Sheridan

SAS 'SHOOT' CHARLES DI SCARED WITLESS

It shows the IRA could murder, kidnap anytime

By Marion Scott

PRINCE Charles was 'shot' and Princess Diana and her two Royal sons kidnapped by a terrorist hit squad in an exercise that scared Di witless.

The terrifying war game at the Royals' Scottish home, Balmoral, was what sent her rushing back to Buckingham Palace less than 36 hours after arriving in Scotland.

Pundits thought her sudden change of mind signalled a rift in the Royal marriage. But really it was sheer terror.

The exercise involved local police, SAS, and a crack London police bodyguard squad from the Met.

It was to test security at Balmoral and at Birkhall, which is now being used by the young Royals.

It was staged less than a week before Di and Charles arrived at Birkhall with Prince William and Prince Harry for their holiday.

The Royals insisted on being told the fate of their "stand-ins" by embarrassed security chiefs.

An insider revealed: "The Princess was scared stiff. When she announced that she was leaving none of us was surprised."

In the exercise a mock IRA hit squad attacked the Royal estate from the hills south of Balmoral.

ALLIGATOR EATS CAR!

A GOBSMACKED Texan teenager couldn't believe his eyes when an ALLIGATOR tried to EAT his CAR!

It crawled into the road while stunned John Collins, 18, was driving home.

The 'gator opened its jaws and SANK its TEETH into one of the tyres.

FLYING DOG GETS LUCKY

MOTORIST Donald Barbrook, 71, was gobsmacked when a FLYING DOG smashed through his windscreen.

The mutt was being chased by an Alsatian in Funtington, near Chichester.

It landed in Donald's lap, then leapt out and ran off – unhurt!

HE KEPT WIFE CHAINED

A JEALOUS husband was so frightened randy rivals would steal his wife he chained her to the central heating every time he went out.

And it went on for YEARS.

"When we used to go out for walks together even a sideways glance would make him mad, said attractive Mrs Dusty Milosaljevic after her escape from bondage.

"If a man wolf-whistled there was a fight, he was so insanely jealous."

Dusty's husband Bosko moved his family to Sweden ten years ago — but he couldn't get used to the free-loving way of life there.

After eight years of being chained up, mother-of-two Dusty, 35, made a try for freedom.

She wandered round their high-rise suburb in Malmo — "but I might just

HIGH-RISE flat where Bosko (inset) imprisoned his wife Dusty

as well have been on Mars," she said.

"I couldn't speak a word of the language. Bosko found me wandering lost in a park and I got a beating I'll never forget."

An interpreter translated her incredible story and police found Bosko, 35, out hunting for her.

"I only did it because I love her," he told them. "Men were always making filthy suggestions to her."

He'll now go on trial for causing Dusty grievous bodily harm.

Megablob Micky

■ MEGABLOB blubberguts Micky Mounds ate so much his stomach BLEW APART at the seams!

■ And when the giant food junkie looked at his waistline he saw FIVE gaping holes oozing fat.

■ The 65-stone slob scoffed until he couldn't stand. When he stood up his knees buckled under his incredible bulk.

■ His vital statistics were a mind-boggling 118-inch hips, 1156-inch waist and 91-inch chest.

■ And SEX was a big FLOP for the enormous American fattie. He couldn't even SEE his manhood under his frightening folds of flab.

■ Micky, 35, went on a crash diet and now weighs a meagre slim-line 26 stone.

Moo-sic

SINGING farmer Ken Prestidge has sold his cows in a bid for stardom.

He cashed in his 35 pedigree Jersey milkers to cut his first single, Love at First Sight.

"You could say I've diversified to beat the milk quotas," the Carmarthen, Dyfed farmer said.

Egyptian ghost stops star Linda going mad!

HOLLYWOOD superstar Linda Evans told last night how a 35,000-year-old Egyptian GHOST saved her from MADNESS!

Her crack-up crisis came when ex-husband and film producer John married glamour goddess Bo Derek.

The Dynasty star confessed she was on the verge of an emotional breakdown and, in desperation, sought psychiatrist help.

But the best medical minds in America could not help the blonde bombshell in her darkest hour, so she turned to renowned psychic medium Judy Knight, an authority on the spirit world.

A mystical Egyptian spirit guide called Ramtha, who Judy could conjure up at will tapped into the WISDOM of the AGES.

"She told me I had to defend my psyche and fight back when others tried to attack and destroy my identity," said Linda.

"The instruction she gave me were crystal clear. It was like looking in a mirror and seeing my own reflection giving me advice."

Bells hell

A PHANTOM bell-ringer is making life hell for villagers with midnight visits to their church.

The spectre baffles locals by regularly giving his unwelcome performances at St Mary and St Nicholas, in Saunderton, Bucks — then vanishing before investigation.

BURIED IN DOG GRAVE!

A BUNGLING funeral director discovered he had mixed up a customer's coffin with the one his pet dog was in . . .

And as a result the man ended up in the pets' cemetery, and his St Bernard was sent to be cremated.

Grieving relatives weeping at the crematorium did not know they were seeing off a dog.

Later on staff at the pets' cemetery buried Mr Bert Bosley — alone and unlamented.

Funeral director Judd Orlando discovered the ghastly error when he was putting the ashes into an urn for Mr Bosley's widow.

"I found the metal dog collar and tag," he said. " I realised with horror that I had cremated the dog and buried his owner."

Widow, Mrs Mary Bosley, 51, said: "I was furious with Orlando.

"My poor husband wanted to be cremated when he died — instead he went into a dog's grave.

Her daughter Lois added: "We all gathered round my father's pine coffin and prayed before it was taken into the fire.

"It's horrible to think we were praying while Dad was being buried all alone like that."

Mrs Bosley said: "Bert was killed in a car smash and Rocky the dog was with him.

"He was devoted to Rocky, he's had

. . . as wife sees dog cremated

him for ten years. And he'd bought a plot at the pets' cemetery for him.

"I asked Orlando to take care of both bodies. I thought Bert would rest in peace if he knew his beloved companion was taken care of."

A red-faced Orlando said: "They were both about the same size, so I thought it would be nice to put them in identical pine coffins.

"No one ever looked inside the boxes before the ceremonies, of course."

Orlando, whose business is in Melbourne, Australia, has promised the family he will have Mr Bosley exhumed and give him a proper cremation service.

TUNA TROUBLE

AN EVIL hubby HACKED his wife to death with a rusty TIN-OPENER... because she couldn't open a can of lunch time tuna fish for him, in Florida.

BEAM ME UP MA'AM I WANT TO BE KING

iT'S UFOs by Royal Appointment — Head-in-the-Stars Prince Charles has joined a galaxy of celebrity space-watchers who believe in little green men.

He's at the centre of a new cosmic controversy after graciously accepting weirdo sci-fi novels by the founder of the evil Scientology cult L. Ron Hubbard.

The mystical Hubbard trilogy Mission Earth — stories of futuristic heroes zapping across the universe in flying saucers — is now sitting on one of the Prince's personal bookshelves in Buckingham Palace.

Charles, who has been buzzed by UFOs on a trans-Atlantic flight, is not going to throw them out, according to the Palace, even though author Hubbard was banned from Britain in 1968 when Scientology was branded as sick and dangerous by the Government.

The plant-loving Prince got his aide Lieut. Brian Anderson to write back to publishers of Mission Earth saying "thanks for the kind thought". The Palace admitted that it

By Howard Sounes

WASN'T a standard reply and they do censor what the Prince receives in the post.

Hubbard, who died at his California mansion retreat recently, was at the centre of the brain-washing cult. But his corrupting works are still by Royal Command.

Buzzed

The wacky Prince is becoming obsessed by extra-terrestrial life forms after encountering "a glowing red object" that buzzed his DC10 as he returned from a trip to the USA nine months ago.

After his close encounter, the Prince told friends: "I'm convinced what we saw was a monstrous craft. It appeared like a giant lighthouse bea-

Prince ... sent thanks

con hanging in the sky.

"I felt I was in the presence of something outside our knowledge and control."

Prince Philip, too, has a passion for the unexplained. The crusty duke once invited a sky-watcher who had witnessed a UFO landing to visit Buckingham Palace and tell his story.

Pooches pine for Liberace

CAMP pianist Liberace's 23 dogs are still pining for the star more than a year after he died of AIDS.

The heartbroken hounds still haven't forgotten the expensive luxuries — including champagne — lavished on them by their beloved owner.

As the millionaire lay gasping on his death-bed, his only concern was for the pack of pampered pooches.

And he personally asked his housekeeper of 36 years, Gladys Luckie, to treat them like royalty until they too panted their last.

"I often can't sleep at night because of the tortured howls I hear from Liberace's place," said a neighbour near the star's Palm Springs mansion.

"They were never like that before he died. I suppose they really miss him — he loved them like children.

"There are a lot of people crying out for the money Liberace left behind, but at least the dogs are crying for him."

The housewives' heart-throb was convinced he would one day be reunited with the crestfallen canines in heaven.

"I love dogs more than people. Dogs are helpless and they only want love," he said.

Bush bog gets the bum's rush

FRENCH president Francois Mitterrand has caused an international stink... by slagging off George Bush's BOG.

The toffee-nosed Leftie gave the US president's comfort station the BUM'S RUSH because the POT was too high for his BOT.

George's wife, Barbara, was FLUSHED with anger when Mitterrand turned his nose up at her toilet.

The champagne socialist — who lives like a king in a Paris palace — sent out a team of aides to check over the Bushes' country retreat before a vital summit meeting between the two leaders.

Then fancypants Francois regally ordered the Bushes to:

● RIP OFF a raised-level bog seat that had been specially installed for George's elderly mum;

● Put in a huge BONKING bed for him and his wife, Danielle, at the house in Maine.

"This whole thing got on Barbara's nerves. She's been livid all week," said a source close to the First Lady.

And sheepish George admitted: "She bawled me out about that!"

GHOST JAILS ARMED THIEF

By Andrew Baxter

BURGLAR David Harvey began a seven-year sentence this week — haunted by the portrait of a man who died 200 years ago.

For it was the ghost of royal engraver William Woolett that put him behind bars.

The picture was among family heirlooms that Harvey, aged 42, stole from the home of farmer Alan Secrett at Milford, Surrey.

Harvey was disturbed by Mr Secrett and threatened him with a gun and a knife.

But the ghost picture brought a sweet revenge.

The portrait, of a distant uncle of the farmer's wife, was sold to the owner of a London Gallery, an expert on the 18th Century engraver for a collector in America, who was one of his descendants.

But when collector William Woolett flew in from the States he recognised it instantly as one that used to hang on the wall at the home of his sister . . . Mrs Secrett.

Inquiries by police led to Harvey's arrest at a hotel in London.

The amazing story of the portrait that put the finger on Harvey unfolded at Guildford Crown Court, Surrey.

Forced

It began when Mr Secrett came home for lunch to find the robber upstairs in a bedroom.

His first words were "I've got a gun. I've got a knife. Do as you are told. You know what happens to people who don't."

Mr Secrett said he was forced down the stairs and told to rip out the telephone wires before being locked in the lavatory.

Mr Secrett said he was determined to catch Harvey somehow and memorised an accurate description to give police.

King's tomb

ELVIS fans are planning to honour him by building a £25m replica of Egypt's Great Pyramid with 20,000 seats and a museum, near Presley's former home in Memphis.

OLD TIME GHOST GIGS ROCK PAIR

BILL and Joy Kerkhoff get a free music hall show in their home every night — thanks to a couple of SINGING SPOOKS!

The songs are regularly belted out by the spirits of an old theatrical couple who used to live at the Kerkhoffs' home.

Applause

Applause and whistling from a PHANTOM audience add to the atmosphere, as old favourites such as Keep Right On To The End Of The Road resound through their flat in Radbourne Street, Derby, in the early hours of the morning.

At first, Bill thought the music came from a neighbour's radio but when he went to complain, he was told about the ghostly performances.

Bill said: "I like my friendly ghosts. I don't want them disturbed by anybody."

Say cheese . . . at the loo

THE owner of a former public loo wants a pizza the action . . . by turning it into an Italian takeaway.

But his planning application kicked up a stink with the parish council in Hayfield, Derbyshire.

"I wouldn't like to buy anything to eat from an ex-gent's toilet," snorted Cllr. Kathleen Waterhouse.

Now the local planning authority must decide if the idea is topping . . . or just half-baked.